FROM THEORY TO PRACTICE IN SOCIAL WORK

For the students who took part in the research

From Theory to Practice in Social Work

The development of social work students' practice

JENNY SECKER
Research Officer
Fife Social Work Department

Avebury

Aldershot · Brookfield USA · Hong Kong · Singapore · Sydney

Published by
Avebury
Ashgate Publishing Limited
Gower House
Croft Road
Aldershot
Hants GU11 3HR
England

Ashgate Publishing Company
Old Post Road
Brookfield
Vermont 05036
USA

A CIP catalogue record for this book is available from the British Library and the US Library of Congress.

ISBN 1 85628 400 X

Printed and Bound in Great Britain by
Athenaeum Press Ltd., Newcastle upon Tyne.

Contents

Acknowledgements   vi

1   Introduction and overview   1

2   Aims and methods   4

3   The typology of approaches to practice   24

4   The everyday social approach   30

5   The fragmented approach   46

6   The fluent approach   78

7   The part played by academic teaching   105

8   The part played by practice placements   117

9   Questions, answers and more questions   137

Bibliography   142

Acknowledgements

My first debt of gratitude is to the students who took part in this research, not only for the time they committed to the project despite the other pressures they faced, but also for the thoughtfulness with which they approached the task of exploring their experiences with me. In small repayment of a large debt this book is dedicated to them. I am also very grateful to the supervisors of the research, Professor John Triseliotis and Mrs Lorraine Waterhouse, for encouraging me to develop my own ideas and for offering constructive criticism of earlier drafts of the material presented here.

Amongst the many other people who contributed less directly but no less essentially I am particularly grateful to my family in London, who gave me much support and encouragement, to my friends who sustained my belief in the possibility of understanding others and of being understood in turn, and to my husband, Roger, for his persistent belief that I could and would achieve what I set out to achieve.

1 Introduction and overview

The origins of this research lay in a proposal submitted to the Economic and Social Research Council by the Department of Social Policy and Social Work at Edinburgh University. The proposal was submitted in 1987 against a background of imminent change in the pattern of education and training for social work which highlighted the lack of any detailed evaluation of either current or previous patterns of training. Since the changes being considered by the Central Council for Education and Training in Social Work were in part a response to perceived public anxiety about how adequately students are prepared for practice, a central objective of the proposed research was to contribute to the development of methods for the monitoring and evaluation of training programmes.

In the original proposal it was envisaged that this objective would be achieved through the design of an instrument for the measurement of social work students' performance. The instrument was intended to be used with students at key stages of their education and training in order to ascertain the relationship between their performance, their background characteristics and their mode of training. By implication, then, the proposed research strategy involved a pre-test / post-test experimental design and a statistical analysis of multi-variate correlations. Accordingly, in the early stages of the project the work undertaken consisted largely in exploring the problems and possibilities involved in designing an appropriate performance measure. The conclusion drawn, however, was that the reliability and validity of a performance measure for use in this educational field would remain in doubt, and that more might be achieved by exploring the possibilities afforded by a qualitative, descriptive research strategy. In the following chapter the rationale behind this decision is explained in more detail. The questions which it was hoped to address through adopting a qualitative, descriptive strategy are then discussed with reference to the literature of social work education and other relevant fields, before describing the way in which the strategy was implemented.

The purpose of Chapter Three is to provide a bridge between the discussion of aims and methods in the preceding chapter and the presentation in the following chapters of a typology of three approaches to social work practice, which might be described as the heart of the research findings. The information provided in Chapter Three covers the terminology used to describe the three approaches, their distribution across the different stages of training at which the students who took part in the research were interviewed, some caveats about the meaning of the typology, and some issues which have either been set aside for discussion in later chapters or omitted altogether.

Having provided this background information, each of the three approaches to practice which constitute the typology are described in turn in Chapters Four, Five and Six. In order to facilitate a comparison of the three approaches each chapter follows broadly the same outline. An overview of the approach under consideration is presented first, with particular reference to the sort of knowledge on which the students drew in the context of that approach. The approach in question is then described in more detail from the perspective of the ways in which the students went about obtaining and interpreting information about situations they encountered in practice. Finally, their approach to helping the people with whom they worked is examined.

A central premise which underpins the typology of approaches is that it represents a model within which the development of the students' practice as they progressed through training can be understood. Having identified the three approaches, the part played by the students' education and training in the development of their practice can therefore be explored. In Chapter Seven the part played by academic teaching is examined with reference to the influence both of course content and of the different teaching approaches employed. In Chapter Eight the part played by the students' placement experiences is then considered. The kind of approaches to practice teaching which appear to have been unhelpful and helpful to them are described first, while an analysis of the part played by a range of factors associated with their placement agencies concludes the chapter.

Following the presentation of the research findings in Chapters Four to Eight, the focus of the concluding chapter shifts back to the aims discussed in Chapter Two. The information generated in relation to the questions it was hoped to address is assessed, and issues which might be addressed by future research are identified.

Before moving on to the research aims and methods, two caveats should be inserted here. The first concerns the implications of the changes which have been a feature of social work education and training over the past few years. As was noted earlier, the funding proposal in which the research originated was submitted at a time when the Central Council for Education and Training in Social Work was planning major changes in the pattern of training. Although the Council's plans to replace the existing qualifications in social work and social service with a single qualification obtained after three rather than two years' training were eventually rejected by central government, the intervening years have nevertheless been a time of rapid change. The implementation of an alternative strategy also involving the development of a new single qualification is now well advanced. In addition, the implementation of plans for the accreditation of practice teachers and the approval of placement agencies are also well under way. As a result of this latter development in particular, some of the questions raised by this research about the quality of social work education and training may now be being addressed.

Secondly, even setting aside developments in national training policy the course which is the focus of this study has not stood still. On the contrary, a rather different curriculum leading to a different academic qualification has been developed, while less visible changes may also have taken place as both academic and practice teaching approaches have developed in the natural way of things. For this reason the course depicted here may bear little resemblance to its present day counterpart.

2 Aims and methods

The aims of the research

The primary aim of this research was to ascertain whether different approaches to practice could be identified on the basis of social work students' accounts of their work, thus making a contribution to the development of methods for the monitoring and evaluation of social work education. As was seen in the previous chapter, although the objective of making a contribution to the development of evaluative methods was central to the funding proposal in which the research originated, it was envisaged that this would be achieved through the design of an instrument for the measurement of students' performance at key stages of their education and training. The problems encountered in attempting to pursue this strategy therefore require some examination here in order to explain why it was thought that students' accounts of their work might provide more useful information.

An examination of the literature relating to educational evaluation reveals that the type of experimental strategy originally envisaged represents a long established approach. Tyler (1947), for example, describes three stages in the evaluative process: the definition of educational objectives; the design of a performance measure based on those objectives; and the appraisal of students' performance in terms of the measure at strategic points of their educational experience. Other writers, however, have highlighted the limitations of the experimental design, and have argue for greater use of qualitative, descriptive methods. In a widely cited contribution to the literature of educational evaluation Parlett and Hamilton (1972) suggest, for example, that educational objectives alone offer an inadequate basis for an evaluation, since they represent only an idealised version of an undertaking which in practice may be open to interpretation. The authors go on to argue for the inclusion of qualitative methods in a broadly based strategy which they term illuminative evaluation.

A second argument, put forward by Patton (1980), concerns the problems involved in establishing the reliability and validity of a performance measure. Patton suggests that in fields where performance measures have not been carefully designed and thoroughly tested more accurate results can be obtained by documenting what students can do and actually have done than by relying on their responses to a standardised test the reliability and validity of which are suspect.

These arguments were influential in shaping the aims of this study, because in the course of developing the research it became apparent firstly that social work education is a field in which educational objectives are peculiarly open to interpretation, and secondly that this situation has implications for the reliability and validity of any performance measure.

That educational objectives in the field of social work education are open to interpretation is illustrated by the existence of long standing debates both about the role and purpose of the profession, and about the knowledge and skills required for practice. These debates are well documented and require little elaboration here. While the arguments put forward in the Barclay Report (National Institute for Social Work, 1982) illustrate the different views which pertain about the roles and tasks to be undertaken by social workers, the different positions taken by Sheldon (1978), Jordan (1978) and England (1986) illustrate the extent of debate about the kind of knowledge on which social workers should draw. Clearly, the design of a performance measure based on such disputed objectives presents a formidable task.

It might be argued, however, that the consensus about the competencies required of qualifying students recently reached in developing the new Diploma in Social Work offers a way forward. That this is not the case stems from the fact that the competencies listed in Paper 30 (CCETSW, 1989a) are only broadly described, perhaps in part as a result of the difficulties involved in constructing a consensus from amongst such a diversity of opinion. In turn implications arise for the reliability and validity of any performance measure designed around the agreed competencies.

Miller and Wilson (1983) define reliability as the extent to which a measure would give consistent results if applied to the same people either more than once or by different raters. The same authors define validity as the extent to which an instrument really measures what the researcher set out to measure. The problem, then, is one of achieving a sufficient degree of standardisation while at the same time ensuring that what is being measured is not distorted.

Writing in the context of performance evaluation in the field of occupational psychology, Landy (1985) advises that standardisation can be achieved by breaking down broadly defined areas of competence into clearly defined constituent parts which are then described by criteria the presence or absence of which can be readily recognised by raters. In addition the consistency of the criteria across the different situations

5

encountered within a particular occupation must be ascertained. In the field of social work education, however, despite the consensus recently achieved about the competencies required of qualifying students, the implementation of either of these two steps poses problems.

In the first place, although some of the more concrete competencies arrived at in developing the Diploma in Social Work might quite readily be broken down and described in terms of criteria by which they can be recognised, the majority seem unlikely to be susceptible to such treatment. Moreover, it is questionable whether even criteria describing the more concrete competencies would hold good across the varied contexts of social work practice. The following 'catch all' clause illustrates, for example, the extent to which the definition and recognition of criteria to describe the core skills listed in Paper 30 would depend on complex judgements about what is appropriate in a remarkably wide range of circumstances:

> Skills will also need to be selected and combined appropriately in relation to the task being undertaken, to the needs and wishes of the participants, to the availability of other demands and resources, to the setting and circumstances, and to the numbers of people involved. (CCETSW, 1989a, p.16)

Despite these problems, researchers in the United States have made extensive use of the experimental design, particularly in evaluating the effectiveness of focussed skills training formats. As the following examination of seven of these studies, undertaken by Fischer (1975), Clubok (1978), Schinke et al. (1978 and 1980) Shapiro et al.(1980) Larsen and Hepworth (1982), and Kopp and Butterfield (1985), indicates, however, in order to achieve an acceptable level of reliability the researchers concerned have sacrificed the validity of their performance measures.

Focussed skills training formats appear to lend themselves well to experimental evaluation both because they emphasise the development of highly specific skills described in terms of the behaviours required for their use, and because the required behaviours are practised by students in standardised role played simulations. As a result, in the seven studies in question the problem of ensuring reliability was relatively easily overcome by using these standardised simulations to operationalise a performance measure designed to assess students' skill levels before and after training. In all seven cases the students' skills were found to have improved after training. Because their aim was to evaluate the effectiveness of training in developing students' practice skills the validity of these studies depends, however, on the extent to which skills developed and demonstrated through the medium of role played simulations are transferred to practice. Amongst the researchers concerned, only Kopp and Butterfield appear to have questioned the assumption that this is the case.

Initially, Kopp and Butterfield employed video-taped role plays both as training materials, and to operationalise a performance measure in a pre-test / post-test experimental design. In common with other researchers, they found that students' skill levels appeared to improve after training. Unlike other researchers, however, Kopp and Butterfield carried out a further test designed to ascertain whether the skills apparently acquired during training were transferred to practice. This test is of particular interest because on this occasion, despite the problems of reliability which they acknowledge, the researchers employed video-taped recordings of students' work with clients to operationalise their performance measure. They found not only that the skills acquired in training did not transfer to practice, but also that a homogeneity of style which developed amongst the student sample during training dissipated in the field.

Kopp and Butterfield offer a number of explanations for these findings, including the possibility that work with clients involves complexities which are not reflected in role played situations. If this is the case, however, then their study demonstrates in addition that in the field of social work education the design of a standardised and therefore reliable performance measure is likely to place the validity of the measure in doubt. This conclusion is supported by two previous reviews of a wider range of North American research than can be encompassed here. Both Bloom (1976), who reviewed fifty studies, and Sowers-Hoag and Thyer (1985), who reviewed a further twenty two studies, conclude that more attention has been paid to the reliability of the performance measures employed than to their validity.

Given that the present research originated in the need to develop evaluative methods in order to address concerns about the extent to which students are prepared for practice, to replicate the approach of North American researchers seemed insufficient. A decision was therefore taken to examine the possibilities afforded by a qualitative, descriptive strategy. It was through exploring what has been achieved in the fields of occupational psychology and nursing studies by using this kind of strategy that the aim of ascertaining whether different approaches to social work practice could be described on the basis of students' accounts of their work emerged. In both fields researchers have employed a technique known as critical incident technique to ground descriptions of different levels of performance in the accounts either of observers or of practitioners themselves.

Flanagan (1954) locates the origin of the critical incident technique in a series of studies undertaken by North American psychologists during the second world war with the aim of developing procedures for the selection and classification of aircrews. The main thrust of the studies he describes was to obtain more specific information about the kinds of behaviours which differentiated effective and ineffective performance of the tasks required of wartime pilots than was contained in the generalised explanations commonly given for failure, such as 'unsuitable temperament', or 'poor judgement'. In order to obtain more specific information, personnel who were in a position to directly observe pilots' actions were

7

asked to describe incidents during which a pilot had acted in ways which were especially helpful or unhelpful in accomplishing a particular task. Behaviours which were observed to have contributed to the accomplishment of a task were termed the critical requirements of that task.

Within the field of nursing studies the kind of techniques described by Flanagan have been closely replicated by Jenson (1960) and more recently by Cunningham (1981). Jenson's study aimed to explore the potential of the critical incident technique for describing the requirements of effective nursing. Twenty one supervisors, senior nurses and staff nurses were asked to record information about the behaviour of a nurse whom they believed to be especially ineffective and to repeat the exercise in relation to a nurse whom they believed to be especially effective. On the basis of his analysis of this information Jenson compiled a classification of the critical requirements of nursing which include personal, professional and social skills. Similarly, Cunningham asked a group of ward sisters and charge nurses to observe the behaviour of staff nurses in their wards and to classify the behaviour observed as effective or ineffective. She went on to use the information obtained to relate changes in nurses' performance to changes in their workload.

These studies, then, have in common with those described by Flanagan a reliance on observations of behaviour for the generation of information about the critical requirements of the work under consideration. As a result, their emphasis has been on the description of observable interpersonal and technical skills, while the less observable cognitive background against which those skills are deployed is left out of focus. In the fields of both occupational psychology and nursing studies, however, critical incident techniques have been adapted to describe cognitive as well as behavioural and interpersonal skills. In both fields this has involved the prior nomination of expert practitioners by managers, peers and consumers. The nominated experts are asked to provide detailed accounts of their approach to a particular piece of work. Their accounts are then compared with those of other practitioners not nominated as experts in order to describe those features which distinguish the work of experts.

In the field of occupational psychology this strategy has been termed job competency assessment. Klemp and McClelland (1986) describe the use of the strategy to identify the characteristics of intelligent functioning amongst senior managers. Staff and clients of the organisation which commissioned the study were asked to identify managers whose work they regarded as exceptional. Both these nominated experts and other managers whose work was regarded as less exceptional were asked to select a piece of work which they considered to be successful and to describe their approach to that piece of work in considerable detail. Transcripts of these interviews were then analysed by readers who were not aware which accounts were those of the nominated experts. Having first identified themes which appeared to distinguish outstanding performance from more average performance, the readers went on to identify thought processes and techniques which indicated the presence of those themes. Klemp and McClelland note that the accounts of the managers who had been nominated as experts were indeed distinguished on this basis from other accounts.

In the field of nursing studies Benner (1984) employed a similar strategy to explore the development of expertise in nursing. Benner interviewed 120 senior nurses who had been nominated as experts by their superiors and peers and 120 newly qualified nurses for whose supervision these senior nurses were responsible. Each senior and junior nurse was asked to describe independently their approach to the nursing care of a patient with whom both had worked. Using this material, together with further material obtained from interviews with other nurses at a range of levels of seniority, Benner was able to describe five approaches to clinical work, ranging from that of the novice to that of the expert. Some of the distinguishing features she describes will be considered later, since they have some significance for the aims of this research.

In considering how the techniques outlined above might contribute to the development of methods for the monitoring and evaluation of social work education an approach with the capacity to explore cognitive processes seemed likely to prove most useful because, as will be seen shortly, the knowledge used by social workers and the ways in which that knowledge is used are issues of considerable concern in this field. The strategies employed by Klemp and McClelland and Benner were therefore of particular interest. It seemed inappropriate, however, simply to replicate their methods because, in comparison with the occupations they studied, social work is a peculiarly private undertaking. In contrast with nursing, for example, a great deal of social work practice takes place not in a public arena such as a hospital ward, but in the context of private encounters between worker and client. For this reason Pithouse (1987), who undertook a study of a local authority child care team, describes social work as an 'invisible trade'. He found that the privacy which surrounds social work practice created difficulties for senior social workers in supervising the work of basic grade staff, and notes that these difficulties were compounded by an egalitarian culture within which all qualified workers were deemed to be equally competent. Under these circumstances, the identification of expert social workers seemed likely to prove both difficult and contentious. Although Harrison (1987) obtained the assistance of staff at the National Institute of Social Work in identifying 'excellent' workers for the purposes of a study which will be examined further later, he does not make it clear on what basis they made their selection. In a field where the nature and purpose of practice are a matter of considerable debate any basis for the selection of experts is, however, likely to be open to dispute.

Nevertheless, the idea of grounding descriptions of different approaches to practice in the accounts of practitioners appeared to have considerable potential. In particular, it suggested the possibility of obtaining accounts of

9

practice from social work students as they progressed through training in order to ascertain whether different approaches to practice could be described in terms of their knowledge and skills. In turn, were this to prove possible, it would become possible to use the information obtained to achieve a second aim: that of exploring the influence of different aspects of their education and training on the students' approaches to practice. Although no detailed monitoring and evaluation of social work training has been undertaken in Britain, those studies which have been undertaken suggested that the influence of both academic and practice teaching might repay further exploration.

As far as academic teaching is concerned, previous research has generated concern about the relationship between the theoretical material taught on courses and social work practice. In addition to the findings of two surveys of the views of former students, which reveal considerable dissatisfaction with the academic content of courses leading to the Certificate of Qualification in Social Work (Davies, 1984; Gibbs and Gygno; 1986), a further four studies based on interviews with qualified practitioners suggest that social workers make little use of the theory taught on these courses (DHSS, 1978; Carew, 1979; Corby, 1982; Waterhouse,1987).

Although these findings have generated considerable concern amongst social work educators, their findings are not unproblematic. While survey methods are able to provide only limited information, with the result that the reasons behind respondents' dissatisfaction with academic teaching remain unknown, the conclusions drawn by other researchers about the extent to which social workers make use of theory in practice are based on some questionable assumptions. The interviews conducted by Stevenson and Parsloe for the DHSS, in common with those conducted by Carew and Waterhouse, reflect, for example, an assumption that to use theory properly social workers must be able to clearly articulate their knowledge in the form of propositions recognisably derived from the relevant literature. Similarly, because Corby's interview schedule was based on a commonly prescribed problem solving format involving assessment followed by intervention and evaluation, his conclusions clearly rest on the assumption that this format represents the only correct way of using theory in practice.

The findings of a further study undertaken by Barbour (1984) which would appear both to support and offer an explanation for the conclusions drawn by other researchers are also problematic. Using the techniques of participant observation in conjunction with interviews, Barbour aimed to explore the process of professional socialisation in social work as it was manifested amongst one class of students. She reports that although the ideal of using theory in practice was initially a high priority amongst the students, their efforts towards attaining this goal were hampered by their perspectives on social work practice. While some students, particularly at the beginning of training, thought of practice as a 'helping' process, later in training more students began to conceive of it as a process of 'healing'. Barbour suggests that from the perspective of 'helping' theoretical material was viewed as a set of directly applicable procedures, akin to recipes, and that the students perceived their course to be deficient in providing this kind of knowledge. From the 'healing' perspective, on the other hand, greater standing was ascribed to the personal traits of practitioners than to theoretical material, and the need for professional training was consequently held in doubt. On this basis she concludes that the answer to the problematic relationship between theory and practice identified by other researchers lies in selecting students who would bring to training a more appropriate perspective on practice.

Although this study seems, then, to support and explain the findings of other studies, Barbour appears to take at face value the accounts offered by the students in whose training she participated and to assume that they were an accurate representation of the students' approach to the use of theory in practice. In doing so, she does not appear to consider an alternative interpretation suggested by other studies of professional socialisation such as those undertaken by Becker et al. (1977) and Melia (1987), that changes in the students' accounts might reflect a concern on their part to gain approval in the academic setting by expressing views perceived to concur with those of their teachers. In the light of these studies, it seems at least possible that an increasing tendency to express a 'healing' perspective on the part of the students in whose training Barbour participated could have been encouraged by an emphasis amongst the teachers concerned on a therapeutic approach to practice, since such an approach, although rather unfashionable now, might still have been influential in the late 1970s and early 1980s when Barbour's study was undertaken.

In summary, then, it is arguable that what previous research demonstrates is not that little use is made of theory in practice, but that theory appears not to be used in accordance with the assumptions of the researchers. In fact, as Paley (1987) points out, a re-examination of the findings of some of these studies reveals that respondents have not said that theory is of no use to them at all. Rather they have given some remarkably similar accounts of its use, to the effect that it provides 'a framework' for practice (Carew; DHSS), is 'integrated' with or 'assimilated' into practice (Carew; Barbour), and that different theories or aspects of them which seem relevant to a particular situation are 'amalgamated' and used as seems appropriate. (Stevenson and Parsloe; Barbour). These explanations suggest that theory may be more widely used in practice than has been supposed, and that further exploration of its use and of the implications for social work education is required.

Some support for this conclusion can be found in the work of a number of writers who have rejected commonly held assumptions about the use of theory in practice. Although not directly concerned with social work practice, Schon (1983) offers a particularly cogent critique. Skilled practitioners, he argues, do not solve problems in the stepwise, assessment

11

followed by intervention fashion commonly prescribed within the professions. Rather they engage in what he terms a 'reflective conversation', in the course of which the situation to hand is framed and reframed in the light of a practitioner's repertoire of possible explanations and solutions. Depending on how satisfying a picture emerges, these explanations and solutions are themselves adapted until a satisfying solution, which is at the same time an explanation, is found. Schon describes this process as reflection-in-action. When a satisfying solution for a situation is found, he suggests, it is added to the practitioner's repertoire of ways of understanding and resolving problematic situations, to be modified and adapted in turn as new situations are encountered. From this perspective, then, skilled practitioners are seen as researchers who develop their own stock of theories through experience.

Within the field of social work education this kind of conceptualisation of the practitioner as theory builder seems to be gaining some ground. Evans (1987) and Gould (1989) both argue, for example, that rather than concentrating on imparting knowledge to students, social work educators should focus on enabling them to derive theories from their experiences of practice. However, England (1986) takes a somewhat different position. He proposes that the kind of theoretical knowledge taught on social work courses can enhance social workers' understanding of the situations they encounter. In his view, though, it cannot do so in the form of discrete sets of propositions which in themselves purport to offer a complete explanation for human situations. Instead, England suggests, theory constitutes a stock of knowledge to be 'plundered and fragmented' (p.35) to inform an essentially intuitive understanding of the diverse situations encountered in practice.

In his later work on educating the reflective practitioner Schon (1987) also suggests that experimentation with preconceived rules and ideas may be a necessary stage in the development of skilful practice:

Perhaps we learn to reflect-in-action by learning first to recognize and apply standard rules, facts and operations; then to reason from general rules to problematic cases in ways characteristic of the profession; and only then to develop and test new forms of understanding and action where familiar categories and ways of thinking fail. (p.40)

There would appear to be some consonance between this view of the relationship between theory and practice and the findings reported by Benner (1984) and Harrison (1987), whose work was briefly discussed earlier. On the basis of her analysis of the accounts of nursing practice she obtained, Benner concludes that only novice nurses relied on preconceived rules and theories to guide their work. In contrast with the rather laboured, rule following approach which resulted, more experienced nurses relied increasingly on ways of understanding and responding to clinical situations developed through and grounded in their experience as preconceived ideas were challenged and reframed. Benner terms these ways of understanding situations 'paradigm cases'. Not dissimilarly, Harrison found that when asked about the knowledge on which they drew the twenty five 'excellent' social workers who took part in his research indicated that they selectively used knowledge derived from the social sciences, together with other sources of knowledge, to construct conceptual frameworks and ideas about how to practice.

Harrison's study appears to be the only study undertaken in Britain to have explored the knowledge used by social workers without importing prior assumptions about its use. An exploration of social work students' approaches to practice at different stages of training therefore seemed likely to contribute further to understanding in this area. In particular, if the kind of knowledge commonly described as theoretical is not used in the form of discrete sets of propositions but is plundered, assimilated, or used as a framework to guide the generation of new theories grounded in experience, then, it was thought, it might be possible to catch something of the process involved 'on the hop' as it were, as students are exposed to this kind of knowledge in the course of their education and training.

Much of the teaching on social work courses is provided, however, not in the academic institution but in practice agencies, and this teaching also seemed likely to repay exploration. In particular, four previous studies suggested that it would be useful to explore the influence of different approaches to practice teaching on the development of students' practice. The first of these studies was undertaken in the United States by Rosenblatt and Mayer (1975), who obtained accounts from 233 students of practice situations which they had found particularly stressful. An analysis of fifty of these accounts revealed that the stressful situations described by the students concerned had involved experiences of four practice teaching approaches which they found objectionable. Predominant amongst these approaches was a 'therapeutic' approach within which problems encountered in practice were attributed to deficiencies in a student's personality, and attempts made to address their deficiencies by exploring them in supervision. While this approach raised the most strenuous objections, three further approaches were also considered objectionable. These included a 'constrictive' approach involving the curtailment of the students' autonomy by teachers who imposed their own theoretical perspective on their students' work; an 'unsupportive' approach, characterised by aloofness, coldness and even hostility on the part of the practice teacher; and an 'amorphous' approach within which too little direction was provided by the teacher. Because their focus was on stressful situations, Rosenblatt and Mayer are unable to provide very much information about practice teaching approaches which were perceived to be helpful. They do note, however, that a warm, supportive approach had enabled some students to cope with other stressful experiences during their placement.

There would appear to be some overlap between the findings of three studies undertaken in Britain and those reported by Rosenblatt and Mayer.

13

One of these studies, undertaken by Michael (1976), explored practice teaching content and method through the medium of a multi-faceted research strategy involving participant observation, semi-structured interviews and written questionnaires. On the basis of a comparison between the information generated by interviews with thirty practice teachers and the descriptions offered by students of 'good' and 'bad' supervision, Michael delineated two approaches to practice teaching which were informed by the teachers' own models of social work practice and which students found unhelpful. These she describes as an 'apprenticeship / administrative and technical' approach, which placed emphasis on the acquisition of administrative and technical skills, and an 'apprenticeship / growth' approach, where the focus was on students' emotional growth and self awareness. Like the students interviewed by Rosenblatt and Mayer, then, the students questioned by Michael found practice teaching approaches based on their teachers' own model of practice or directed at their personal and emotional growth unhelpful. Michael was also able, however, to provide information about a third approach which the students found more helpful. She describes this approach as an 'educational contract' approach. In the context of this approach, she suggests, the aims of a placement were governed not by the teachers' own model of practice, but by the educational needs of their students.

A second study of practice teaching in the British context was undertaken by Syson and Baginsky (1981). Using a semi-structured schedule the authors interviewed practice teachers, students and tutors who had been involved in forty one placements. Perhaps because obtaining students' perspectives on practice teaching constituted only one aspect of a broader aim, that of providing a profile of practice placements in Great Britain, Syson and Baginsky were unable to identify particular practice teaching styles. They do, however, present a number of comments made by students which again have some consonance with the findings reported by Rosenblatt and Mayer. One student, for example, complained of supervision sessions which were no more than weekly reporting sessions, suggesting an amorphous approach. Other students felt that their practice teachers had been impersonal and overly professional, suggesting an unsupportive approach. In addition, although almost all this sample of practice teachers thought a therapeutic approach unacceptable, one student thought a teacher had attempted to employ too psychoanalytical a approach, while another complained of too great an emphasis on the discussion of feelings.

The unacceptibility of a therapeutic approach amongst the practice teachers interviewed by Syson and Baginsky probably reflects a move within the field of social work education away from what Curnock (1985, p.78) describes as 'social working' students, following criticism of this kind of approach. However, the view that practice skills are entirely inappropriate in practice teaching is challenged by a third small scale study undertaken by Brodie (1990). Brodie's study was based on an analysis of tape recordings of eighteen supervision sessions, involving six practice teachers and their six students, which were supplemented by interviews with both parties. Although his focus was primarily on the content of practice teaching, and particularly on the extent to which teachers make explicit reference to theoretical ideas, Brodie found that the use of certain skills commonly associated with practice, such as encouraging exploration, summarising and clarifying, was appreciated by students. He also identified an approach employed by two teachers which their students found unhelpful and which he terms a 'caseload management' approach. Like the 'reporting sessions' complained of by one student to Syson and Baginsky, this approach would appear to bear some resemblance to the amorphous approach described by Rosenblatt and Mayer.

These studies, then, have yielded some interesting information both about the kind of approaches to practice teaching which students find objectionable, and about approaches which they say are more helpful. It cannot be assumed, however, that teaching approaches which students find objectionable are necessarily unhelpful for the development of their practice, nor that approaches they say are more helpful do in fact have a beneficial influence on their practice. This question was therefore one which it seemed might usefully be explored in the context of a longitudinal study of students' approaches to practice.

The methods employed to achieve the twin aims of the research are the focus of the remainder of this chapter.

The research methods

It will be apparent from the earlier discussion that it was something of a foregone conclusion, arrived at on the basis of the work of previous researchers, that interviews with social work students would be the method used to achieve the aims of the research. However, this choice of method raises three questions which require some discussion before going on to describe how the research strategy was implemented.

Firstly, a review of some contributions to the methodological literature of the social sciences suggested the need to develop a clear conceptual perspective from which to undertake the research, in order to avoid importing preconceptions about the knowledge and skills required for practice. As Cicourel (1964, pp.222-223) points out, unless an explicit conceptual perspective is developed, the way in which information is treated will depend on an implicit model within which the observations made and inferences drawn are likely to interact in unknown ways with the researcher's own biographical situation. This caveat seemed particularly apposite in view of my background as a former social work student and practitioner, which seemed likely to lead to an analysis based on my own views about social work education and practice.

After considering the strengths and limitations of different perspectives in relation to the aims of the research, the position I adopted was one informed by the phenomenological sociology of Alfred Schutz (1970), whose focus, in contrast with that of other writers on describing an external reality, was on the interpretative procedures by means of which we construct our own subjective reality. One strength of this perspective lay in the fact that rather than relying exclusively, as previous researchers have done, on what respondents say about the knowledge on which they draw, students' accounts of their work could be analysed to yield information about knowledge on which their work was based, but which they themselves might not be able to articulate in response to direct questioning.

A further strength of the perspective lay in providing a stance from which to explore and analyse students' work while minimising the intrusion of preconceptions. Garfinkel (1967), who took Schutz's work as his own starting point, explains that a phenomenological enquiry should be undertaken from a stance which regards the phenomena under investigation as 'anthropologically strange'. By this he means that the researcher should not simply assume that familiar interpretations of familiar situations are adequate. Instead, familiar situations should be treated as if they are unfamiliar in order to reveal the usually unremarked ways in which they are constructed. Amongst previous researchers, Dingwall (1977) adopted a not dissimilar stance towards the ways in which health visitor students made sense of their education and training, as did Oleson and Whittaker (1968) in exploring the ways in which student nurses accommodated and integrated the multiple roles and selves involved in becoming both adult members of society and members of their profession.

Alongside these strengths the phenomenological approach also has limitations. These revolve around the fact that the conclusions drawn by the researcher inevitably rest on a re-interpretation of respondents' own interpretation of events. It is not possible, therefore, to claim with any certainty that the same conclusions drawn by one researcher would be drawn by another, nor that those conclusions are applicable to situations other than the unique situations they describe. A phenomenological perspective cannot, then, be regarded as a panacea for the problems of reliability and validity which were encountered in considering the adequacy of an experimental design, and my decision to adopt this perspective was not, therefore, made on the grounds of a greater claim on truth or reality. Rather it was made on the grounds that the approach offered a more appropriate way of contributing to the development of evaluative methods in the field of social work education than was offered by the experimental design, given the uncertainty which prevails in this field about educational objectives. Although the research might leave unanswered questions about other possible interpretations of the information obtained and about the generalisability of the conclusions drawn, it would at least demonstrate what could be achieved using qualitative methods, and provide a basis for further exploration.

The second question raised by the choice of interviews with students as the research method concerns the extent to which students' accounts of their work can be regarded as accurate versions of that work. It was suggested earlier, for example, that the accounts obtained by Barbour (1984) may have been constructed to meet the perceived expectations of social work teachers. Equally, it could not be assumed that the accounts obtained in the course of this research had not been constructed to a particular end. In addressing this problem the position taken by Garfinkel (1967) again proved helpful. Garfinkel points out that to question whether a respondent's interpretation of events is accurate is to make an unfounded assumption that another source of data would have a greater claim on reality. In the context of this research, for example, I might have attempted to corroborate students' accounts of their work by observing their practice, on the erroneous assumption that my interpretations of what I observed were more accurate than the students' own accounts. Given that this kind of assumption is unfounded, Garfinkel goes on to argue that the questions raised by the use of accounts as a source of data revolve not around their internal validity, since to pose that question is to assume the possibility of a more accurate version, but around the researcher's treatment of them. He does not suggest, however, that respondents' accounts be taken at face value, as Barbour seems to have done. Rather, he proposes that they can be treated as versions of reality which make sense in their own context. Hence the task of the researcher is not to appeal to other sources of knowledge to question or corroborate an account, but to reach an understanding of how it makes sense in the context in which it is offered. From this perspective students' accounts of their work can, then, be accepted as a valid source of information, with the proviso that in interpreting them the question must be raised and addressed as to why a particular account is offered in a particular context.

The final question raised by the choice of research method concerns whether the use of a combination of sources of information might not have been more appropriate. Denzin (1978) suggests, for example, that the use of multiple sources, which he terms triangulation, can offer a more complete picture of a research area than one source alone, and most writers appear to agree on this point, providing that different sources are used to provide complementary layers of information rather than to question or corroborate one another. In view of this general agreement, the decision to limit the scope of the research to one method was based not on any theoretical objection, but on practical considerations. I anticipated, correctly as it turned out, that the kind of longitudinal, exploratory study of students' approaches to practice I envisaged would generate a large amount of material for analysis. If that analysis was to be accomplished within the constraints of the time and resources available, it seemed wiser to accept the limitations of a strategy employing only one method than to embark on the development of a second strand to the study. In short, the advice offered by Patton (1987) seemed apposite:

> Triangulation is ideal. ... But in the real world of limited resources attempts at triangulation may mean a series of poorly implemented methods rather than one approach well implemented. (p.61)

Nevertheless, it has to be acknowledged that a second source of information about students' different approaches to practice would have been useful. In particular, as a number of studies have demonstrated, consumers' views can shed much light on the extent to which social workers' activities are perceived to be helpful by the people they are intended to help (Mayer and Timms, 1970; Rees and Wallace, 1982; Sainsbury et al., 1982; Howe, 1989). In the absence of this kind of information, the contribution made by this research to the development of methods for the monitoring and evaluation of social work education is somewhat circumscribed, since it cannot be claimed with any certainty that the typology of approaches to practice which resulted represents a hierarchy of performance levels, in the sense of one approach being more helpful than another to the consumer. The meaning which can be attached to the typology is examined in the following chapter. In the meantime the way in which the research strategy was implemented requires some description here.

As with the decision to rely on only one source of information, the implementation of the strategy involved balancing theoretical ideals with practical considerations. On this basis it was decided that the study should take the form of an exploration of the practice of two groups of students, drawn from consecutive cohorts, who were undertaking one social work course. The course chosen as the focus of study was a two year postgraduate course which was offered by the department within which the research was undertaken and which led to the Certificate of Qualification in Social Work. The advantages of focussing on this particular course lay partly in the accessibility of the students concerned, and partly in the concern of teaching staff in the department to begin to develop methods of evaluation by focussing on their own work rather than on that of other teachers. The following description of the course draws on the outline provided for students.

During the first year, in addition to a practice placement undertaken concurrently with the second and third academic terms, teaching was provided in social policy, sociology, psychology, human development and principles and practice of social work. Both group and individual tutorials were also provided. The course in principles and practice of social work was divided into two parts. Part One aimed to provide both a broad grounding in social work theory, practice and skills, and an introductory framework applicable to a wide range of methods and settings. The teaching methods used included lectures, talks by practitioners, exercises and discussions in small groups, and role play, including, in the second term, the use of audio-visual equipment. Part Two covered social work in residential and day care settings and social work with families. Between the end of the first academic year and the beginning of the autumn term the students undertook a second, full time practice placement lasting ten weeks.

The second year of the course included, in addition to continuing group and individual tutorials, courses covering the following areas: social work practice; social work and social philosophy; social need, social policy and social work practice; psychology, human development and psychiatry; organisational analysis and change; law and social work; and the transition to work. In addition to this wide range of courses the students were asked to opt for one specialist class, and to select a number of topics for study in a series of professional practice seminars. The course in social work practice covered group work, mental health and psycho-sexual counselling, and social work practice with children and young people. The course in social need, social policy and social work practice included community work, children in care and substitute care, a three-day conference on ethnicity and social work, social work with older people and their families, a two-day conference on child abuse and teaching on addictions. The range of teaching methods used again included lectures, role play, the use of audio-visual equipment, talks by practitioners and small group discussions. A final concurrent practice placement was undertaken from the second half of the autumn term until the end of the academic year.

This course, then, was fairly typical of many courses leading to a qualification in social work, in that it aimed to cover a wide range of material from an equally wide range of perspectives.

Although it would have been ideal to have interviewed all the students who took part in the research at the beginning of training and at the end of each year of their course, which coincided with the end of their first and final practice placements, it was not possible to do so within the time scale of the research. Instead, ten students drawn from a cohort already in training were interviewed towards the end of their first and final placements, while a further eleven students drawn from the following cohort were interviewed at the beginning of training and towards the end of their first placement. Because two of this second group suspended training during their second year only nine of the eleven students were interviewed for a third time towards the end of their final placement. A total of fifty one interviews were therefore conducted over a period of time which spanned three academic years.

Prior to their first interview the twenty one students who took part in the research were asked to complete a questionnaire designed to obtain information about their age, previous experiences of practice and educational background, including whether they had previously studied three subjects commonly thought relevant for social work: sociology, psychology and social policy. On the basis of their responses the following information was compiled.

In age, the students ranged from twenty two to thirty six years old at the beginning of training, the average age amongst them being twenty seven years. The length of their previous social work experience ranged from that of one student who had a year's experience of voluntary work, to that of three students who had between eight and thirteen years' experience obtained largely in paid employment. The average length of previous experience was just under four and a half years.

Fourteen students had gained all their experience in residential and day care settings, while three students, in addition to some experience in these settings, had been employed more recently as trainees or assistants in local authority area teams. Of the remaining students, three had gained their experience working in either a voluntary or paid capacity with community based projects providing services for people with needs relating to mental health or ageing, while one student had specialised in working with adolescents. Seven students had gained all their experience in one job, while fourteen had held two or more posts.

As far as their educational background is concerned, four students had obtained an ordinary degree, one student had obtained a third class degree, nine had obtained a lower second, and seven an upper second. None of the students who took part in the research had obtained a first class degree. Eleven students had studied one or more of the three subjects thought relevant for social work as part of their undergraduate degree course, and a further four had studied one or more at school or since their degree. Six students had not previously studied any of these subjects.

The interview schedule developed to explore the students' approaches to practice was designed to achieve a balance between an approach so structured that little scope remained for them to describe their work in their own way, and one so unstructured as to impede the achievement of the aims of the research. In order to provide a clear focus, each interview concentrated on the students' recent work with one particular client or group, although the schedule was sufficiently flexible to allow for comparisons between different pieces of work.

The choice of work was left to the students, but questions designed to ascertain the basis of their choice were included in the schedule. From the information obtained it emerged that their choice was made not on the basis of concerns about being seen to be successful, but on the basis of a concern to provide sufficient 'meat' for discussion. In their view short term work, involving only one or two meetings with clients, was not appropriate material. Consequently the focus of the research is on their longer term work and excludes, in particular, the short term assessment of need and provision of material resources. With this exception, a wide variety of work was discussed, including work undertaken in area team settings and residential, group and community work.

The framework of the interview schedule and the more specific lines of questioning pursued were developed in the course of a series of eight pilot interviews conducted with social work students who were undertaking a one year course of education and training within the same department as the students who subsequently took part in the research proper. This exercise proved invaluable, since despite the experience of previous researchers my anxiety about having some formal structure initially resulted in an attempt to divide the interview schedule into areas covering assessment, decision making, and intervention, following the commonly prescribed problem solving framework used by Corby (1982). Like Corby's respondents, however, the students who took part in the pilot interviews experienced difficulty in describing their work within this framework.

On listening to recordings of the pilot interviews it seemed that this difficulty arose because from the students' perspective their work had not been structured along the lines of a problem solving format, but had evolved more in the manner of a story unfolding as time elapsed. In order to take this perspective into account I redesigned the interview schedule using a simple story structure involving a beginning, a middle and an end. The beginning segment was further divided in order to explore the students' approach prior to meeting the people with whom they worked for the first time as well as their approach to their first meeting. This story like framework proved more helpful in enabling the students to describe their work, although some students continued to experience difficulties which will be discussed when the findings are presented. Depending in part on how much difficulty was experienced, but also on the complexity of the work described, the length of the interviews varied considerably from one and a half to four hours. In some cases it was necessary to conduct the longer interviews in two stages, either because of constraints on the students' time, or in order to avoid exhaustion for both participants.

The pilot interviews were also helpful in identifying useful questions. After asking the students to describe a segment of their work in detail eight lines of questioning were pursued before moving onto the next segment. These included: how the students had made sense of the information they had obtained; what skills or abilities they had drawn on in the course of the interactions they had described; what had contributed to each of these facets of their approach; how they had felt about undertaking the work; what their own preoccupations had been; how clear they had felt about what they were doing; whether anything had been particularly helpful to them; and whether they thought anything could have helped them more. Before exploring the ending of each piece of work a further set of questions was asked. These concerned the students' overall understanding of the situation they had described, how they had arrived at that understanding, and, again, what had contributed, been helpful or might have helped in that process.

These basic lines of questioning were augmented as the research developed in the light of the students' responses so that particular patterns of responses could be explored further. For example, during the first set of research interviews three students indicated that written work, such as case notes and summaries, had been helpful to them in undertaking the work they described. In order to explore this further a question about the usefulness or otherwise of written work was added to the interview schedule and yielded some interesting information. Developments in each

21

student's practice were also explored by including in the schedule questions about whether their approach would have been different at an earlier stage of training, together with questions designed to address particular issues which had been explored during previous interviews with the same student.

In addition to these questions, the final section of the interview schedule contained questions about what the students perceived as the successes and failures of their work, about what they had learnt and identified as future learning needs, and about what they understood to be the hallmarks of a good social worker. Questions were also included here to directly address their perceptions of their education and training. Within the broad framework provided by the schedule the students were free to describe their work in their own way, while I was also free to pursue interesting lines of enquiry until a particular subject seemed to be exhausted.

All the interviews were tape-recorded with the students' permission, and with the guarantee that their identity and that of the other people discussed in the course of the interviews would remain confidential. In accordance with this guarantee the names of the people and places concerned have been either omitted or changed in presenting the research findings in subsequent chapters. The tape recordings were later transcribed by myself. Although this was a time consuming and somewhat tedious process the opportunity to reflect on each interview by reliving it, as it were, was helpful both in continuing to develop useful interviewing techniques and in beginning to analyse the material obtained.

The analysis took the form described by Silverman (1985, p.11) as an inductive analysis, and followed the guide lines offered by Becker (1971). Although these guide lines were of considerable assistance, it would be inaccurate to convey the impression that I was able to put the inductive method into practice smoothly and without hitch. On the contrary, the process of analysing the interview transcripts was often quite bewildering, since it proved all too easy to become lost in a maze of information which seemed idiosyncratic and disconnected. This problem was compounded by the fact that the interviews which generated the material for analysis were conducted at several points in time, with the result that a great deal of uncertainty about the eventual conclusions had to be contained while the analysis of the first transcripts proceeded. Often my anxiety about reaching some more certain conclusions intruded, resulting in a rather black and white approach which was no sooner translated onto paper than it was swept aside. Moreover, the elation of every insight gained was swiftly followed by the onerous task of completely rethinking previous conclusions in the light of a new perspective. It would probably be more accurate to describe my experience of the inductive method as one of discovering what was involved through encountering problems and having to resolve them, than to suggest that it involved only the orderly implementation of a tried and tested set of guide lines.

Eventually, however, after a great deal of drafting and re-drafting, followed by an equally lengthy process of fine tuning, I was able to construct a cohesive model to describe and explain the information I had obtained. The basis of this model consists in the typology of three approaches to social work practice which are described in turn in Chapters Four, Five and Six. Before describing each approach, some more general points about the typology are discussed in the following chapter.

3 The typology of approaches to practice

In describing the three approaches to practice which constitute the typology it has been necessary in the interests of clarity to present a somewhat stereotypical picture of each approach. Inevitably, some aspects of the information obtained in the course of the research therefore had to be set aside, either temporarily or altogether. As a result readers may find themselves wondering, for example, about the range of approaches deployed by students at the same stage of training, about what has become of some of the issues explored in the course of the research, or about the absence of topics which seem relevant to a particular theme. The main aim of this chapter is therefore to bridge these gaps by providing a range of information intended to assist in making sense of the following three chapters. First, though, the terminology used to describe the three approaches requires some explanation.

The terminology used to describe the three approaches

The three approaches to practice were distinguished on the basis of the knowledge which underpinned each approach and the ways in which that knowledge was used. These distinguishing features are reflected in the name given each approach. Hence the approach described in the following chapter is termed the 'everyday social approach' to reflect the fact that in the context of this approach the students did not draw at all on the kind of knowledge which is usually described as theoretical. Instead they drew solely on knowledge derived from their personal, everyday social lives. In turn, the term 'fragmented' was chosen for the approach described in Chapter Five, because in the context of this approach the students' practice was characterised by conflicts between their everyday and theoretical knowledge which resulted in dilemmas about how to act in the course of interactions with clients and others. On similar grounds, the third approach in the typology is termed the 'fluent approach', because in the context of this approach the students were able to creatively amalgamate different sources of knowledge, thus resolving the dilemmas which characterised the fragmented approach.

The distribution of the three approaches

Although the typology of approaches represents a model within which the development of the students' practice as they progressed through training can be understood, their progress from one approach to another was by no means related solely to their stage of training. Information about the distribution of the three approaches across the different stages of training at which the students were interviewed is presented in Table 1 below. As the table illustrates, nine of the fifty one accounts of practice obtained in the course of the research depicted an everyday social approach, thirty three depicted a fragmented approach and nine depicted a fluent approach. While six of the eleven students interviewed at the beginning of training had deployed an everyday social approach prior to training, five had deployed a fragmented approach. None of the students interviewed at this stage had deployed a fluent approach. By the end of the first placement, however, this pattern of distribution had changed. Only two of the twenty one students interviewed at this stage had deployed an everyday social approach, while sixteen students had deployed a fragmented approach. In addition three students had deployed a fluent approach. Towards the end of training the distribution of the three approaches had again changed slightly. At this stage only one student had deployed an everyday social approach, twelve students had deployed a fragmented approach and six students had deployed a fluent approach.

Table 1
Distribution of approaches to practice across three stages of training

	Prior to training	First placement	Final placement	Total
Everyday social approach	6	2	1	9
Fragmented approach	5	16	12	33
Fluent approach	0	3	6	9

An analysis of the students' accounts suggests that the rather patchy and idiosyncratic pattern of development reflected in Table 1 was closely associated with their placement experiences, the significance of which is discussed in Chapter Eight. In the meantime, in order to clarify the educational context of the material presented in the following chapters, where extracts have been drawn from the students' accounts to illustrate the three approaches the stage of training of the student concerned has been noted at the end of each extract.

The meaning of the typology

Although insufficient information is available about the relative helpfulness of the three approaches to practice to claim with any certainty that the typology represents a hierarchy of performance levels, it is nevertheless arguable, on more limited grounds, that the development of a fluent approach to practice can be regarded as representing a desirable educational objective. As will be seen in Chapter Six, it was only in the context of this approach that the students were able to sustain work based, though by no means exclusively, on the kind of theoretical material taught during their course. It should be made clear here, however, that the figures presented above cannot be regarded as a measure of the overall success or otherwise of the course in question in enabling students to develop a fluent approach to practice, because no attempt was made to secure a representative or random sample of students.

A further caveat about the meaning of the typology concerns the point made earlier about the somewhat stereotypical picture presented of each approach to practice. In effect, the lines of demarcation which have been drawn between the three approaches to practice are rather more clear cut than were the students' accounts of their work. In reality, some of the students' accounts depict a degree of movement away from the approach with which they have been included towards the next approach in the typology, while others retain vestiges of the preceding approach. Amongst the nine accounts which have been included with the everyday social approach, for example, only the six accounts obtained from students at the beginning of training were entirely typical of the approach. In the remaining three cases, as the students' work developed they began to move away from the everyday social approach. Equally, of the thirty three accounts which have been included with the fragmented approach only fifteen were entirely typical of the approach. In the other seventeen cases the students had been able to resolve some of the problems associated with the fragmented approach, but continued to experience sufficient problems for their accounts to be included with that approach. A further three students, however, were able to resolve all the problems associated with the fragmented approach in the course of the work they described, and their accounts have therefore been included amongst the nine which depicted a fluent approach.

Although much of the description of the three approaches to practice contained in the following chapters is based on those accounts which were most typical of each approach, the more marginal cases were also of particular interest because they revealed a great deal both about the approach with which they have been included, and about the other approach which they most closely resembled. For this reason extracts from these accounts have on occasion been used to illustrate more than one approach.

Issues set aside in describing the three approaches

Four issues which were explored in the course of the research interviews have been set aside either temporarily or altogether in the three chapters which follow. The first concerns the approaches to practice deployed prior to training by the eleven students who were interviewed at the beginning of their course. As was seen above, while six students had deployed an everyday social approach, five had deployed a fragmented approach. The reasons behind the differences reflected in these figures have not been discussed in the following chapters because the focus of the research was on qualifying training. It can be noted here, however, that differences in the students' approach at this stage appeared to be associated with the extent to which supervision, in-service training or agency ethos had introduced them to ways of working which differed from the ways in which they approached their everyday social lives.

A second issue which has been set set aside in the following chapters concerns the part played in the development of the students' practice by their own background characteristics. Although information about the students' educational background, age and length of previous experience was obtained with the intention of exploring this issue in some detail, for the most part these characteristics appear to have had little relevance. The level of degree obtained by the students does not appear, for example, to have had any bearing on the development of a fluent approach to practice, since the degrees obtained by the nine students who had developed a fluent approach by the end of training spanned the range obtained by the students who took part in the research. Similarly, previous study of the three academic subjects thought relevant for social work - sociology, psychology and social policy - does not appear to have been advantageous, since seven of the nine students who developed a fluent approach had studied none of these subjects. However, the students' age and length of previous experience may have made some difference, in that some of the older, more experienced students who took part in the research encountered difficulties which appear to have been related to these characteristics. Because the difficulties they encountered were associated particularly with their placement experiences they have been set aside for discussion in

Chapter Eight.

The third issue which has been set aside in the following chapters concerns the use of what might be termed role specific knowledge; that is the kind of knowledge about legal and bureaucratic procedures which was relevant within a specific agency or to a particular type of work. As Jordan (1982) points out, a great deal of social work practice is governed by legal and bureaucratic procedures, and a degree of conflict exists within the field about the extent to which this is desirable. Under these circumstances it might seem rather strange that this type of knowledge has not been mentioned in describing the three approaches to practice, and it may therefore be helpful to explain that omission here.

In fact, two themes did emerge from the students' accounts in relation to their use of role specific knowledge. As far as the first of these themes is concerned, it can be briefly noted that the students frequently experienced a great deal of anxiety when embarking on the work they described about the procedures which should be followed. Although this anxiety contributed to some of the difficulties they described, particularly in the context of the fragmented approach, in comparison with other sources of anxiety it quickly abated. In short, it appears that the role specific knowledge required to carry out their work was relatively readily grasped, and that once grasped it was no longer a cause for acute concern. For this reason this theme has been set aside in the following chapters in order to focus on the more protracted difficulties experienced by the students.

Underlying this first theme, however, was a second theme which revolved around the influence of different policies and procedures on the students' approach to their work, and hence on the development of their practice. This theme has been only temporarily set aside in the following chapters. It will be brought back into focus in Chapter Eight and considered there in relation to the learning milieux provided by the agencies under whose auspices the students worked.

The final issue which has not been included in the following chapters concerns the endings of the students' work. This topic has been set aside altogether, because by the end of their first placement there was very little difference in the way in which the students approached ending their work, regardless of which approach to practice they had deployed. Their accounts suggest that this was due to academic teaching in the early stages of their course, which appears to have resulted in a persistently uniform approach. To summarise this approach, during both their first and final placements the students were concerned to be clear with the people with whom they worked about the time scale of their work. As the time for leaving approached they then began to discuss the implications in more detail, and in the course of their final meetings with the people concerned they were at pains to review the work which had been undertaken. Given the uniformity of their approach, the only difference in the students' accounts of the ending of their work once they had begun training concerned the degree of difficulty they experienced in reviewing their work during their final meetings. As will be seen in Chapter Five, in the context of the fragmented approach the students were themselves dissatisfied with what had been achieved, and for this reason they not infrequently experienced difficulty or discomfort in reviewing their work.

Having provided some information which it is hoped will be of assistance, the three approaches to practice are now described in turn in the following three chapters.

4 The everyday social approach

An overview of the approach

As was seen in the previous chapter, the term 'everyday social' was chosen to describe the approach to practice which is the focus of this chapter because in the context of this approach the knowledge on which the students drew in undertaking the work they described was derived solely from their personal, everyday social lives. While each student's stock of knowledge was in some respects highly individualistic, a number of common themes emerged. In this first section of the chapter an overview of these themes is presented with reference to the ways in which the students made sense of the situations they described and managed their interactions with the people concerned.

In making sense of the situations they described in the context of the everyday social approach, the students drew on two inter-related strands of knowledge: their personal values and beliefs, and their affective responses to the situations in question. In relation to the former, a common theme was their concern to adopt a stance which they described as being 'non-judgemental'. Their explanations suggest that this stance was typical of their approach to social life more generally and that it had been developed through their own family and other life experiences. Some students explained that values developed in this way had been reinforced by a particular political ideology, while others indicated that their religious beliefs had played an important part.

As Leighton et al. (1982) point out, a non-judgemental stance has been widely prescribed in the social work literature as a prerequisite of good practice:

> According to most writers on the theory of social casework, the social worker should avoid 'judging' his client, i.e. it is not part of the social worker's role to categorise the client as a good or bad person or to assess his virtue or vice. (p.49)

The authors go on to observe, however, that in practice it is not so easy to define what is meant by 'non-judgemental', and the accounts of the students who took part in this research support that opinion. In the context of the everyday social approach the espousal of a non-judgemental stance appeared to be equated not with the avoidance of judgements, but with the espousal of positive value judgements and a concomitant rejection of negative judgements. In the course of their accounts, for example, the students often spoke of their concern to focus on the strengths of the people with whom they worked, and in keeping with that concern they referred warmly to them as likeable, interesting individuals. Their emphasis on their own positive stance was reinforced in some cases by asides in which negative judgements were attributed to others, usually other professionals, and rejected.

Intertwined with this positive value stance was an affective source of understanding which was described by some students as empathy and more figuratively by others as 'putting yourself in someone else's shoes'. In common with the non-judgemental approach to which the students aspired, the ability to empathise with clients has been widely associated in the literature of the profession with good social work practice. Keefe (1975, p.69), for example, notes that a capacity for empathy has been found to be an important ingredient of helping relationships in the field of counselling psychology, and goes on to develop a four stage model of its use in social work. The four stages he describes include the accurate perception of the verbal and non-verbal cues of the other, a direct feeling response on the part of the worker, the separation of these feelings from those of the other, and the accurate feeding back to the other of an awareness of his or her feelings.

In the context of the everyday social approach, however, the term empathy appeared to refer to a more everyday fellow feeling or sympathy, on the basis of which the students arrived at conclusions about the feelings and needs of the people with whom they worked. Their accounts suggest that the development of this sense of fellow feeling was closely related to their value stance, in that it had depended initially on their identifying strengths in and growing to like the people concerned. In turn, in arriving at conclusions about the feelings and needs of the people with whom they worked, the students drew on their own imagined response to the situations they were in and interpreted the information they obtained accordingly. In some cases their imagined response was reinforced by reference to life experiences of their own which they compared with the situations of the people with whom they worked. In contrast with Keefe's model, the students neither attempted to separate out their own feelings from those of the people with whom they worked, nor explicitly communicated them in the course of their interactions. Instead they assumed without question that their feelings were entirely consonant with those of the people with whom they worked.

Within the boundaries of this approach, then, the ways in which the students made sense of the situations they described depended on a combination of positive value judgements and sympathetic responses. It was largely through the medium of their face to face interactions with the people with whom they worked, however, that they obtained the information on which they brought to bear these ways of making sense of situations. As a result, the process of making sense of a situation was not a matter of the straightforward development of ideas on the basis of the information available. Rather the students' accounts reveal an influential and reciprocal relationship between the process of making sense of a situation and the management of face to face interactions. On the one hand, the ways in which they interpreted information exerted an influence on the content and process of their interactions. On the other hand, their knowledge about the management of interactions exerted an equal, reciprocal influence both on what information they obtained, and on the ways in which they interpreted that information. In order to lay the groundwork for a more detailed exploration of this relationship an overview will be presented next of the knowledge on which the students based the management of their interactions.

As a corollary of their reliance in making sense of the situations they described on positive value judgements and sympathetic responses, the students' capacity to undertake the work they described depended on the development of warm, harmonious relationships with the people concerned. Accordingly, their primary concern in relation to the management of their interactions was with the climate of those interactions, and in order to create the kind of climate they wanted they drew on their knowledge about how successful social interactions are achieved and maintained. A first theme to emerge from the students' accounts in relation to this knowledge was their concern to present themselves as likeable, friendly individuals. As one student put it: 'It's just all the things you use to establish any relationship. You know, being on your best behaviour, presenting the best side of yourself'. Associated with this concern about the presentation of self was a second concern that their interactions should proceed as smoothly as possible, without awkwardness or embarrassment. To this end the students harnessed their knowledge about how fluent and harmonious social conversations are managed. In particular, two social conventions which govern everyday conversation were brought into play in ensuring the smooth functioning of their interactions.

The first of these conventions has been described by Goffman (1971) as 'taking the line of the other'. In everyday life, Goffman observes, participants typically find themselves agreeing with the views expressed by others, even if their agreement is no more than lip service. To fail to do so, he points out, is to risk loss of face for one or another of the participants, and hence potential embarrassment and discomfort for all. From the students' perspective, then, the expression of agreement and sympathy with their informant's point of view was felt to be essential for the success of their interactions and for the establishment of the kind of relationships they wanted. Unsurprisingly, the avoidance of disagreement was therefore also

32

of paramount concern.

The second conversational convention which governed the students' management of their interactions concerned the avoidance of potentially embarrassing or difficult subjects matters. These subjects included issues such as sexuality and death which are generally considered taboo in the context of ordinary social discourse, as well as other issues which seemed likely to prove difficult or embarrassing in a specific situation. The students' concerns about addressing such subjects emerged from their accounts either in relation to their difficulties in accomplishing particular tasks, or from their responses to questions about issues they mentioned but did not appear to have addressed. In the context of the latter line of questioning one student's explanation that the subject matters he might have addressed but didn't were 'not exactly after dinner conversations' highlighted the sort of concerns involved.

In the context of this approach, then, there was a considerable degree of consonance between the knowledge on which the students drew in making sense of the situations they described and that on which they drew in managing their interactions with the people concerned. In essence, both aspects of their knowledge were consonant with the establishment and maintenance of warm, harmonious relationships with the people with whom they worked. Underpinning those relationships was a world view informed by the students' personal values and life experiences, and by a range of norms and conventions which govern the establishment and maintenance of successful social relations. Having presented this overview, the everyday social approach will now be explored in more detail from the perspective of the ways in which the students obtained and interpreted information about the situations they described.

Obtaining and interpreting information

It was seen in Chapter Two that when asked to describe the role of theoretical knowledge in their practice, social workers have said that it provides 'a framework' for practice. These responses would appear to suggest that in the absence of the kind of knowledge which is commonly described as theoretical such a framework would be lacking. On the contrary, the accounts of social work practice obtained in the course of this research indicate that the everyday knowledge catalogued above can equally well be described as providing a framework for practice. The framework provided was, however, an integral part of the students' ordinary, everyday ways of making sense of and acting in the social world. As such it was not described as a framework, but was taken for granted by the students on the assumption that the ways in which they understood and managed their work were the only reasonable ways of doing so. The implications for their approach to obtaining and interpreting information are examined here along the lines of the story like structure of the research interview schedule. The initial stages of their work, up to and including their first meetings with the people concerned, are considered first. The main themes which emerged from their responses to questions about how their work had proceeded are then examined. Finally their responses to questions about their eventual understanding of the situations they described are considered.

The initial stages of the students' work

The first area covered in the course of the research interviews concerned the students' approach to the information available before they first met with the people with whom they worked. In some cases the students' work took place in a context where little information was available at this stage, and in these cases this line of questioning was less relevant than in others. In those cases where information was available, however, some distinct patterns emerged from the students' accounts, and these patterns were closely associated with the different approaches to practice identified in the course of the research. In the context of the everyday social approach the pattern which emerged was quite distinctive, in that none of the students concerned had considered the meaning of the information available in terms of the situation to hand, but had focussed instead on the potential for developing a warm relationship with the people concerned. In some cases their explanations suggest that they had been too concerned about whether they would be able to establish the kind of relationship they wanted to pay very much attention at all to the available information. As this student put it:

> I must admit, I wasn't really thinking about it in those terms. I was much more worried about how the visit was going to go. You know, whether I would be able to get on with him, whether there would be any awkwardness. I mean I've had cases where getting a conversation going at all has been like pulling teeth. (Beginning student)

In other cases the students had paid more attention to the information available, but their focus in interpreting that information had been on what indications it contained about the potential for establishing the kind of relationship they wanted. For example:

> In the report it said that the mother was concerned about his behaviour, so I thought if she's concerned that probably means she'll be amenable to me being there. Other than that, I remember my supervisor saying this boy's got no boundaries, but I didn't know what that meant. I suppose I should have asked, but I think I was too worried about the reception I was going to get to really pick up on it. (First placement student)

In the earliest stages of their work, then, the students' emphasis on the establishment of a warm, friendly relationship was apparent. This emphasis was echoed in their responses to questions about their aims for their initial meetings with the people with whom they worked. In describing their aims, for example, several students echoed this student's concern to focus on her client's strengths:

> I wanted to approach it with a positive attitude. I hope I'm not, I don't think I'm judgemental about clients. I like to approach things from the point of view that everyone has some strengths. I think it's very important to be non-judgemental. ... I think that comes from living in a small community where you've got to be able to get on with people from all walks of life. I suppose that's why I came on a social work course. It underpins a lot of things, more than just the way I dealt with this case. (First placement student)

When questioned further about more specific aims the students commonly spoke of their concern to be seen as likeable and friendly by the people with whom they were to work. In comparison with this aim the gathering of information was a much lower priority, as this extract illustrates:

> I had my own needs in terms of finding out things, because I was supposed to be assessing this person, but I didn't want to overdo it. I wanted to find out more about her, but at the same time I didn't want to appear incredibly nosy. I wanted to let things follow a flow, so if she talked about things, then we'd discuss it, but I didn't want to force it. ... I suppose I was concerned about how she would see me, whether she would like me or not. I mean nobody likes to be disliked. (First placement student)

This concern that information should emerge as though from ordinary conversation was widely shared. Accordingly, during their first meetings with the people with whom they worked the students' approach to obtaining information was based on the ways in which successful social conversations are managed. In response to questions about the skills on which they had drawn in eliciting information they often expressed surprise at the idea that any skill might have been involved, and the ways of obtaining information which were described consisted in being friendly, sympathetic, and encouraging. For example:

> I don't think I was using any particular skills. It's hard to think of being able to get on with an ordinary family as a skill, though I suppose it might be. To me it was just what I'd do in any situation. Just being friendly and sympathetic, that's all. (Beginning student)

And:

> I don't know if you'd call it a skill. It's just to do with being able to get on with people. I suppose you pick up cues, like I knew when to just nod and smile and when to give him a bit more encouragement. (Beginning student)

The students' emphasis on this kind of encouraging, sympathetic approach was reflected in turn in the ways in which they interpreted the information which emerged in the course of their first meetings. In response to questions about how they had made sense of that information they commonly expressed bewilderment about the meaning of the question. From their perspective, their informants' statements were regarded as straightforward facts of the case which merited sympathy but no further exploration or interpretation. Indeed, to treat them otherwise was perceived to be tantamount to expressing disbelief or disagreement. This student's response to a question about how he had made sense of the information he obtained was not untypical:

I'm not sure what you mean. It seemed pretty straightforward. His mother was very open about everything so there was no need to go into it in great detail or anything. She told me everything there was to tell: He was the youngest child in the family. He had two older brothers that he tended to look up to a bit. His father had died a year or so earlier. Basically she thought he was bored and a bit too easily led, and I had no reason not to believe her. (Beginning student)

The pattern which ensued

The students' unquestioning approach to the information they obtained in the early stages of their work was both a prelude to and a pattern for the remainder of their work. Their accounts indicate that they approached their subsequent meetings with their informants not with the aim of exploring the information already obtained, but with the intention of encouraging their informants to continue to describe their situation as they saw it and as it unfolded in the interval between meetings. An analysis of these accounts suggests that their reliance on their everyday knowledge about the social world precluded any other approach. In response to further questioning, for example, the student quoted above contrasted his approach with an alternative approach suggested by some recent learning. In doing so he revealed the extent to which his acceptance of his informant's views had been based on personal values and responses, the validity of which he had taken for granted:

I don't think it was a logical approach at all, in the sense that when you're doing this course you might think about loss and bereavement and that kind of effect. I wouldn't have related my assessment to those kind of things. I would have related it more to everyday, unscientific, personal response. Whether I thought this lad was ok, how I felt about the family generally. They were just nice, ordinary people, and underneath it all he wasn't such a bad lad either.

In other cases the students' unquestioning acceptance of their informants' statements had been based on an assumption that the way they felt about the situation to hand was entirely consonant with their informant's own feelings. One student, for example, explained why she had seen no reason to explore her client's stated reason for feeling depressed. As she reviewed her work, however, she considered a different interpretation and in doing so she also highlighted the assumptions on which her original ideas had been based:

It's hard to say how I made sense of it. There wasn't anything complicated about it. She told me she was depressed because of being in hospital and I could see how that would make anyone depressed. I've never been in hospital myself, but it's not hard to imagine that it's pretty depressing, especially when you've been such an active, capable person. Though when I think about it maybe there was more to it, because when she did get home she was still depressed. That quite surprised me. Perhaps the thought of going home to a big empty house was a part of it too. (First placement student)

As a further extract from the same account demonstrates, the students' unquestioning approach could also be associated with a reluctance to address issues which might prove difficult or embarrassing:

The more I think about it the more I think I might have missed out on that angle. It's not as if she didn't talk about living alone in the house. The thing was that when she talked about it, it was all tied in with the past, and I didn't want to dwell on that. ... She'd lived with her brother and sister until they died, and if I'm honest I don't think I had the confidence to be able to talk about bereavement and that kind of thing.

An extract from another account illustrates how a similar combination of factors had played a part in shaping a second student's approach to a different situation:

Student I'm not sure how I made sense of it. It was the first time I'd got involved in this kind of professional thing, where you're taking all your own values and what you would want in that situation and using that to help your client. It's just subconscious really isn't it? ... It wasn't difficult to understand him because we were so close in age. The things he talked about were the things anyone would want at his age: a job and a relationship.

J.S. We've talked quite a lot about helping him to find work. What about relationships, was that something you looked at with him?

Student No, I didn't particularly want to get into that. It was already causing a lot of embarrassment at work because of the way he was with the female staff, and I think it would have been much too embarrassing to discuss it. ... Things to do with sexuality and that kind of thing, they're not things you generally talk about are they? (Beginning student)

Overall, the students' descriptions of their meetings with the people with whom they worked depict warm, friendly interactions which they themselves found enjoyable and satisfying. Unsurprisingly, then, they made little reference to differences of opinion with the people with whom they worked. Alongside their friendly, unquestioning approach some students did, however, reach conclusions of their own about the situations they described. One student who was quoted earlier, for example, added this observation to his account of the information he had obtained from his client's mother:

> Mind you, I thought she had a bit of a rosy view of him. She tended to blame other people for what he did. It was all the teacher's fault, or it was his pals who had led him astray. (Beginning student)

This kind of observation was presented by the students in a way which glossed over any incongruity between their own opinion and that of the people with whom they worked. Further questioning revealed that they had not followed up their observations either with the people concerned, or in interpreting the information offered, because to do so might threaten the smooth functioning of their interactions and place their relationship in jeopardy. The same student, for example, explained later why he had not taken up the question of his informant's view of her son:

> **J.S.** What about what you said earlier about her view of him being a bit rosy, did that come up at all?
>
> **Student** No, that never came up. I think basically things were going smoothly. They were very open and willing to work with me and I didn't want to rock the boat.

While conflicts of opinion between themselves and the people with whom they worked caused few problems for the students, they did in some cases encounter conflicts of opinion either between the people with whom they worked and other professionals, or, when they worked with groups of people rather than with individuals, amongst the different individuals involved. Conflicts of opinion between the people with whom they worked and other professionals occurred when the professionals concerned had put forward interpretations of the information available which differed from the views expressed by the people with whom the students worked. Under these circumstances, the students did not treat the conflicting opinions they described as a cause for further exploration, but as a dilemma about whom to believe. In accordance with their emphasis on the strengths and positive characteristics of the people with whom they worked they resolved this kind of dilemma by choosing to believe their point of view. As this extract illustrates, it was in this context that they contrasted their own positive stance with negative value judgements attributed to other professionals:

> The question of alcoholism had come up earlier, actually. There'd been some query about that while he was in hospital, and I'd raised it with him then. He said he liked a drink and he didn't see anything wrong in that, which seemed fair enough to me. I think there was a tendency in

the ward to stereotype people like him, the dirty old man with a drink problem sort of idea. (First placement student)

More problematic, from the students' perspective, were the conflicts of opinion they encountered amongst the people with whom they worked. The accounts of those students who had worked with groups of people rather than with individuals suggest that group interactions were in any case not easily managed in the context of the everyday social approach. As this extract illustrates, when interacting with groups the students found it hard to attend to all the people present, with the result that they tended to engage in dialogue with one person at the expense of paying attention to the views of others:

I found it very difficult to take in everything that was going on. I wanted to be able to stop it like a video so I could look a it frame by frame. I'd find myself focussing on one person and forgetting about the others, then I'd suddenly realise I was getting totally involved with one person. (First placement student)

This kind of problem was compounded when the students encountered conflicts of opinion amongst the people concerned. In these circumstances they again felt obliged to make a decision as to whom to support in order to achieve a resolution and the restoration of harmony. By making such a decision, however, they risked jeopardising their relationship with one party or another. Nevertheless, they did take sides, and their decisions as to whom to support appear to have been influenced by a dynamic which was associated with their position as a newcomer to the groups with whom they worked. As Douglas (1989, p.146) points out, the main concerns of the newcomer to a group are to be accepted, to do what is expected of them and to avoid offending people who have the power to hurt them. These concerns are heightened, he notes, when the group in question is a small, long standing type of group with no formal arrangements for inducting newcomers. The type of groups with whom the students whose accounts are the focus of this chapter had worked were family groups, and from their perspective family groups appear to have been experienced as a particularly cohesive, long standing type of group. Consequently, their concerns were those of the outsider who fears rejection, hostility and scapegoating. This student's description of her feelings about family work was echoed by other students who described this type of work:

I don't know why family work should be so difficult. I suppose it's because they are a family. They know each other so well, every little nuance of the way things are said and done, and you're not a part of that. I suppose there's a fear that they could all gang up on you at once. (First placement student)

Unsurprisingly, in view of these fears, when the students encountered conflicts of opinion amongst family members, their decisions about whom

39

to support were made on the basis of the kind of concerns described by Douglas. Most commonly the conflicts of opinion they encountered arose between parents and their children, and when faced with this situation the students invariably chose to support the parent's point of view, either because this seemed to be what was expected of them, or because from their perspective parents were more powerful than their children and to avoid offending them was therefore paramount. This student, for example, based his decision on what seemed to be expected of him:

> That meeting was the worst, I'd say. It just became a slanging match. His mother was saying it was all his fault and she couldn't cope with him any more and he was shouting at her about wanting new clothes and how his friends' parents bought them new stuff. I was sitting there in the middle of this. There didn't seem to be anything I could say which wouldn't offend one of them or the other. In the end I supported the mother, because she seemed to be looking to me as another adult to back her up. (First placement student)

In this case, on the other hand, the student's decision was based more on his concern to avoid giving offence to his client's parents:

> It was difficult because he didn't think his epilepsy should stop him looking for a job, and he'd held down a job before. His parents were worried though. They said his fits were a lot more frequent that we'd observed them to be in the unit. Some people thought they might be exaggerating his epilepsy because they would lose the attendance allowance they'd been getting since he'd been unemployed. It's a possibility but I don't believe it was true, not knowing the parents. ... The people at work said I should try to find out if it was the money that was worrying them, but I don't see how I could have done without offending them, and I didn't want to destroy the relationship I'd built up with them. (Beginning student)

The students' understanding of the situations they described

It will probably be clear from the preceding discussion that the students' reliance on their everyday knowledge about the social world precluded the possibility of explaining the situations they encountered in terms other than those immediately available on the basis of their informants' opinions and their own judgements as to the worth of those opinions. On the one hand, the norms and conventions of social discourse precluded any exploration of the information offered, other than by means of the kind of cues and encouragement to go on talking associated with everyday conversation. On the other hand, the students' ways of making sense of the social world were so taken for granted that further exploration or explanation seemed unnecessary. As a result, further information tended to emerge in a piecemeal fashion over time as events unfolded and were described by their informants.

40

The students' replies to questions about their eventual understanding of the situations they described reflect this piecemeal emergence of information. Rather than describing any overall understanding, they offered lengthy, anecdotal descriptions of personalities and events which together had the flavour of stream of consciousness accounts of the lives of the people concerned and of their own involvement in those lives. In essence, despite their concern to adopt a non-judgemental stance, their descriptions were couched in terms which portrayed the attributes and behaviour of the people concerned as good or bad, and the information obtained as right or wrong opinions. These responses are hard to document without presenting unwieldy extracts from the students' accounts, but another form of evidence is more readily presented. This emerged from their descriptions of the problems they encountered in writing case notes or summaries of their work. In the context of the everyday social approach, the students' responses to questions about their written work reflected the problems they experienced in structuring information in ways other than those in which it came to hand. This response was one which was echoed by several of the students concerned:

J.S. Some students have said that they found case notes or other written work helpful in making sense of a situation. Did it work that way for you?

Student No I don't think that helped at all. I think that's something I need to look at in the next placement. I found writing case notes one of the hardest things. It took me hours to do them. Every interview it seemed like there was so much to put in. I tended to write a blow by blow account so I wouldn't forget anything which might be important, but I'd write reams and reams and still not get everything in. I think I'm still confused about case notes, what you put in and what you don't. (First placement student)

In the final section of this chapter the ways in which the students attempted to help the people with whom they worked are examined. Although this aspect of their work has been separated out in this way, it is not intended to imply that their attempts to help were in fact separate from the ways in which they obtained and interpreted information, in the sense of the sort of stepwise, assessment followed by intervention model commonly prescribed. On the contrary, their attempts to help were an integral part of their approach, as will be seen in the course of the following discussion.

Helping people in the context of the everyday social approach

An analysis of the nine accounts which depicted an everyday social approach suggests that, as a corollary of their unquestioning approach to the information they obtained, the students' attempts to help the people with whom they worked had depended on the extent to which the people concerned were successful in identifying and addressing their own problems or needs. When the people concerned identified specific problems or needs and suggested ways of addressing them, the students listened sympathetically and unquestioningly encouraged them to implement their ideas. In two cases this approach was unproblematic, at least from the students' perspective, because the people with whom they worked had been successful in addressing the problems they were experiencing. As the following extracts illustrate, both students acknowledged the extent of their dependence on the people concerned:

> It all just happened really. I mean I was thinking, at seventeen would I have talked a lot about how I was really feeling. But she did. I only had to be there and she talked and talked for ages. When she started telling me that about her father I thought oh God, for her sake I hope it works out with him. But I was depending on her a lot. It worked because of her, her and the mother. They were doing it cleverly, not pushing too much one way or the other until eventually he came round. ... If I was starting again I'd try to think a bit more about different ways of doing it. I was just there really, and it worked, but I was lucky. If she hadn't been so capable I wouldn't have had a clue. (First placement student)

And:

> I was lucky with this case. I didn't have to do anything very much because they had plenty of ideas of their own. All I did was give them a bit of encouragement. I'd have to say it was more down to them that he didn't re-offend than anything I did. If they hadn't known what to do I don't think it would have worked out so well. (Beginning student)

The other seven cases which are the focus of this discussion were very much less straightforward than those described by these two students appear to have been. In four cases problems had arisen because the people with whom the students worked had proposed ways of addressing their problems or needs but had been unsuccessful in implementing them, either because their ideas conflicted with the views of other people, or because they had been unable to carry them through. In three of these four cases the students had unquestioningly encouraged the people concerned in their approach. When problems arose, however, their own response had been limited either to some measure of withdrawal from their attempt to help, or to the kind of sympathetic response which might be made by a friend or family member. This student, for example, described how he had given up on his attempt to help when his client's parents had discouraged their son's attempt to find work:

> What should have happened really, I should have put more effort into helping him find voluntary work, but to the best of my knowledge I thought his parents would follow that up. It never occurred to me they would cop out of that. Then it seemed to lose its, it seemed to fizzle out

at that point. It's a shame because for all the work I did nothing really changed. It's something I'm just becoming aware of now, that it was all unresolved, it wasn't really finished. (Beginning student)

Similarly, this student had given up on his attempt to help when his client had been unsuccessful in implementing his plan to give up drinking:

I didn't have any experience or knowledge of that kind of drinking culture. I thought it would be a matter of straightforward steps. I didn't realise how difficult it would be for him and I don't think I gave him nearly enough support. After he'd started drinking again, I didn't know what to do. Things just drifted on and I stopped working with him after a while. (Beginning student)

This student, on the other hand, had responded as a friend might respond when difficulties arose in implementing a plan agreed with her client:

Student She'd said that she wanted to join the group and she seemed keen to go, but she asked me to go with her the first couple of times so I arranged to go round and pick her up. ... When I got there she was still in her night clothes. She said she didn't feel well enough to go, though there didn't seem to be anything particularly wrong with her.

J.S. What did you do when she said that?

Student Well, there wasn't much I could do. I couldn't drag her to the car and force her to go. I just told her to take some Andrews Liver Salts and go back to bed and take care of herself. ... I don't know why I said that. I suppose it's the sort of thing you'd say to a friend. I said I'd come back in a couple of days and maybe she'd feel like going then, but for a long time after that she didn't answer the door to me. (Final placement student)

The fourth case was rather different. Here the student concerned had again unquestioningly agreed with his client's mother about the best way to address the problems she was experiencing, but had been prevented by his practice teacher from doing as she wished:

What happened was, I went round and I was there for ages. His mother told me about all the things he'd done. She didn't try to hide anything. She was saying I don't want him in the house, I want him into care. So I thought that's it then, I'll take him into care, that's what the mother wants. It wasn't until my supervisor said that wasn't on, that you have to consider the child's interests too, that I thought more about it. ... I think I'd been so relieved that she was willing to talk to me that I didn't want to, I don't mean contradict her, but you know, say anything different. (First placement student)

While this account highlights the unquestioning nature of the everyday social approach, it also suggests that the approach was one which could

43

pose problems where statutory work was concerned. As Clark with Asquith (1985, p.36) point out, social workers are expected to balance a commitment to their clients' interests with the interests of other people and of society as a whole, an expectation which is most clearly visible in the statutory duties required of them. The extract presented above suggests that in the context of the everyday social approach the students' unquestioning approach to their informants' views imposed limitations on their capacity to balance the different interests of all those involved. Evidence to support this view is, however, limited, because of the nine accounts of practice which depicted an everyday social approach only this account and one of the less problematic cases described earlier concerned statutory work.

In the remaining three cases which are the focus of this discussion the students encountered problems because the people with whom they worked had not identified any specific problems or needs, but had communicated instead a more general unhappiness, loneliness or depression. In each of these three cases the students had attempted to help as a friend or family member might help, and had found themselves becoming increasingly enmeshed in their client's life. As their work progressed they found themselves spending more and more time with their client, assisting in the day to day running of their lives. This student's description of her response provides an illustration:

> We had a fixed time for my visits but most weeks I saw him more often than that. It was no trouble because I had to go past there anyway on my way home so I could just drop in. ... I felt so sad for him, that seemed to be the basis of it. I just wished he could get something better out of life, and I felt if I could do anything at all, even if it was doing his washing, even if just being there was enough, I always felt why not. (Beginning student)

In the three cases where the students described this level of involvement in a client's life their remit had been to provide support for people whose needs were associated with aging or mental illness, and it might be argued that their concerned, friendly approach was not inappropriate under these circumstances. From the students' own perspective, however, their involvement in the lives of the people concerned was a disturbing, sometimes painful experience. This student's response to a question about aspects of his work which he had found particularly difficult illustrates the kind of feelings they described:

> I found leaving very difficult. Inevitably when you see someone that much - I saw more of her than I've seen of my own family, and so it became part of my life, and I think to a certain extent those threads haven't been broken yet. ... I think if I was starting again I'd want to have more of an idea of that's you, this is me, partly in a self-preservative sort of way. I very much appreciate the time I've got now, I'm feeling a bit bruised, and so I'm grateful for the time, two years to actually look at the way I've been performing. (Beginning student)

Before moving on to describe the second approach to practice identified in the course of the research the main distinguishing features of the everyday social approach are summarised below.

Summary

In this chapter an approach to social work practice based solely on everyday sources of knowledge about the social world has been described. In the context of this approach the main thrust of the knowledge on which the students drew was the establishment of warm, friendly relationships with the people with whom they worked. Accordingly, in making sense of the situations they described they either unquestioningly accepted the information presented to them or, where conflicts of opinion occurred, made judgements as to the worth of the different opinions expressed which were based on their concern for the relationships they had established. Similarly, the students' approach to helping the people with whom they worked was an unquestioning approach. When the people concerned identified specific problems or needs and proposed ways of addressing them, the students encouraged them to implement their ideas without any further exploration. When the people concerned either did not identify specific problems, or experienced difficulty in addressing those they did identify, the students themselves either withdrew from their attempt to help, or responded in the way a friend or family member might respond.

5 The fragmented approach

An overview of the approach

In contrast with the approach described in the previous chapter, in the context of this second approach to practice the students drew on the kind of explanations which are commonly described as theoretical in making sense of the situations they described. In doing so, however, they experienced considerable problems. In this first section of the chapter an overview of the knowledge which differentiated the fragmented approach from the everyday social approach is presented, together with an analysis of the problems experienced by the students.

The analysis of the thirty three accounts which depicted a fragmented approach was a daunting task, not only because they contained a large amount of material, but also because the idiosyncratic nature of much of that material presented considerable difficulties. In the early stages of the analysis these accounts seemed to depict not so much one approach to practice as a collection of approaches within which different strands in some respects ran together and in others diverged. As the analysis progressed, however, it became increasingly clear that these different strands were linked by a common theme, namely a problematic relationship between the different sources of knowledge on which the students drew in making sense of the situations they described and in managing their interactions with the people concerned.

In making sense of the situations they described the students drew on theoretical explanations which spanned the range of those put forward in the literature for inclusion in the knowledge base of the profession. Although little would be achieved by cataloguing this knowledge in full here, it is of interest to note that some explanations occurred much more consistently in the students' accounts than others. In particular, psychodynamic explanations of human development and behaviour were amongst those most frequently mentioned, while ideas derived from a systemic perspective on family dynamics were also frequently mentioned in the context of work with children and their families. In contrast, explanations relating to group dynamics were rarely mentioned, although the students' work commonly involved them with groups of one sort or another. Similarly, behaviourism was very rarely mentioned as a source of understanding. It will be seen in the final section of this chapter, however, that behaviourist ideas were in some cases implicit in the students' approach.

In addition to these theoretical explanations, some students continued to place emphasis on their affective responses to the situations they described as a source of understanding, and their accounts of the relationship between these two sources of knowledge will be examined in the following section of the chapter. In contrast with the everyday social approach, however, in the context of this approach few students referred to their personal values as a having made a direct contribution to their understanding of the situations they described. Instead, they spoke about using theory to look behind or beyond value based responses to the people with whom they worked. As one student put it:

I think it begins with whether you like them or not, but I know it has to go way beyond that in social work. It's something to do with looking behind that, asking why is this person the way they are. That's where the theory comes in I think, though I'm not very good at using it yet. (First placement student)

Although the students did not refer to their personal values as a direct source of understanding, this is not to suggest that they made no reference to values at all. Rather, they referred to their values in terms of principles of practice which had guided the management of their interactions. This shift in emphasis seems to have been associated more with a heightened awareness of the implications of the values they espoused for the management of their interactions than with any fundamental difference in their value stance. Rather than taking for granted the ways in which they managed their interactions, in the context of this approach the students spoke of a conscious concern to act in accordance with the principles of practice to which they aspired.The principles most frequently mentioned in this context included a concern to adopt a non-judgemental stance which at first seemed little different from the value stance which was associated with the everyday social approach. On closer examination, however, what the students meant by being non-judgemental in the context of the fragmented approach seemed to revolve not so much around a concern to focus on the strengths and positive characteristics of the people with whom they worked, as around a concern to allow them to describe their problems and needs in their own terms.Two further principles of practice underpinned this stance. These consisted in a concern to respect the right of the people with whom they worked to self determination, and a concomitant concern to adopt what was described as a non-directive approach. Like the non-judgemental stance to which they referred, these principles of practice have been widely espoused in the field of social work. It will be seen in the course of this discussion, however, that the students encountered problems in putting their principles into practice.

In comparison with the everyday social approach, the students' accounts also depicted a greater awareness of other ways in which they managed their interactions. It was seen in the previous chapter, for example, that in the context of the everyday social approach the students had regarded an ability to pick up cues and to encourage the people with whom they worked to describe their situations as unremarkable and ordinary. In contrast, in the context of the fragmented approach the students were very much more conscious of these abilities. Rather than taking them for granted they were regarded as skills which could be deliberately brought into play. The consonance between ways of making sense of situations and managing interactions which was a hallmark of the everyday social approach was replaced, however, by conflict.

It was through the process of trying to understand why conflicts between ways of making sense of situations and managing interactions occurred in the majority, but not all, those cases where the students referred to the kind of knowledge which is commonly described as theoretical that it became possible to draw a distinction between the fragmented approach and the fluent approach which will be described in the following chapter. The distinction drawn depends not on the content of the students' theoretical knowledge per se, in which respect there was some considerable overlap, but on the ways in which their knowledge was used. Two definitions of the theoretical knowledge to which the students referred were developed to encompass their different approaches. While the definition which pertains to the fluent approach will be set aside for discussion in the following chapter, that pertaining to the fragmented approach requires some discussion here as a prelude to presenting an overview of the conflicts of knowledge associated with the approach.

An analysis of the students' accounts suggested that the term 'ready made theory' might aptly be used to describe the theoretical knowledge on which they drew in the context of the fragmented approach, because the way in which they attempted to use this knowledge involved the direct application of preconceived explanations to the situations they described. These ready made explanations appear to have been handed on to the students largely through the medium of lectures and textbooks, although in some cases they mentioned agencies where a particular way of working was prevalent, or practice teachers who favoured a particular theoretical perspective, as the source of their knowledge. Throughout this chapter, where the term theory is used this ready made knowledge is the type of knowledge to which the term refers.

Although it is a central tenet of this analysis that the origin of the difficulties experienced by the students lay in their reliance on ready made theory, it is not intended to imply that the handing on of this type of knowledge was in itself unhelpful. On the contrary, it will be seen in the following chapter that some students were able to use ready made theory to overcome the difficulties which will be described here. The way in which they did so contrasted sharply, however, with the students' approach to the use of ready made theory in the context of the fragmented approach. In essence, in the context of this approach the students' approach to the use of their theoretical knowledge was an absolutist approach, in the sense that particular explanations for particular types of situation were regarded as mutually exclusive and as either totally correct or incorrect. This absolutist use of theory underpinned two conflicts of knowledge which were the hallmark of the fragmented approach.

The first of these conflicts arose between the students' use of ready made theory in making sense of the situations they described and their everyday knowledge about the ways in which successful social interactions are managed. Conflicts arose between these two strands of knowledge because from the students' perspective the use of theory in practice required a structured approach to the management of interactions which conflicted with their everyday knowledge about the ways in which successful social interactions are managed. As was seen in the previous chapter, this knowledge revolved around ways of ensuring that interactions are free flowing in form and uncontroversial in content. An analysis put forward by Berger and Luckmann (1967) was helpful in shedding further light on this conflict.

In their treatise on the social construction of reality Berger and Luckmann distinguish between two sources of knowledge about acting in the social world: those of primary and secondary socialisation. The authors define primary socialisation as the process through which, as we grow up, we learn how to behave as adult members of society. Secondary socialisation, on the other hand, takes place in the context of any further educational or occupational experiences through which we learn how to behave in more specific adult roles. In the terms offered by this analysis, then, the process through which the students acquired their everyday knowledge about how social interactions are managed can be described as a process of primary socialisation. In turn the process through which they learnt about the use of theory in practice can be viewed as a process of secondary socialisation. That process was most strongly associated with their education and training, although in some cases it was also associated with their pre-training experiences of practice.

Berger and Luckmann go on to point out, however, that knowledge acquired in the process of secondary socialisation must inevitably compete with that acquired in the powerful processes of primary socialisation. Thus, from the students' perspective, their knowledge about how to use theory in practice, acquired in the course of their socialisation as social workers, was in competition with their more everyday knowledge about the management of successful social interactions, and dilemmas ensued as to which line of action should be followed. This conflict between the use of ready made theory and their everyday knowledge about the management of interactions was not, however, the only source of difficulty for the students. In addition their approach to use of ready made theory also conflicted with their interpretation of the principles of practice to which they aspired.

Clark with Asquith (1985) draw attention to the possibility of conflict between the principles of practice espoused by social workers and the theoretical knowledge to which they are introduced in the course of their education and training. In particular, they point out, much of the knowledge encompassed within the social work curriculum consists of determinist theories which sit uneasily with the principle of client self determination. The authors also point out, however, that the right to self determination is not an absolute right. Rather, in the field of social work it may be qualified by the duties incumbent on social workers. Those duties include that of acting in a client's best interests, the definition of which may arguably depend on a professional judgement based on specialised knowledge. The difficulty faced by social workers, Clark with Asquith suggest, is in deciding where the boundary should lie.

It was in negotiating the boundary between rights and duties that many of the students experienced problems. It has already been seen that their approach to the use of ready made theory was an absolutist approach. In addition, they conceived of the right to self determination as an absolute right. As will be seen shortly, when juxtaposed these two absolutist positions led inevitably to conflict.

Taken together, the two sources of conflict described here were associated with an all or nothing approach to the use of theory in practice which emerged from the students' accounts in the form of two distinct patterns. These patterns reflected their different approaches to resolving the conflicts they encountered. In the context of one approach the students acted primarily in accordance with their everyday knowledge about how successful social interactions are managed, which had some consonance with their conceptualisation of the principles of practice to which they aspired. As a result they were able to make use of the ready made theoretical explanations to which they referred only once they were removed from their face to face interactions, with hindsight as it were. In contrast, other students deployed ready made theory as a set of recipe like prescriptions for practice which displaced not only their everyday knowledge about the management of successful social interactions, but also the principles of practice to which they aspired.

These contrasting patterns could perhaps have been separated out and described as two distinct approaches to practice. The students' accounts suggest, however, that they were two sides of the same coin which represent two opposite but related approaches to resolving the conflicts they encountered. In fact, the separation out of the two patterns is in itself something of an analytical device, because in some cases the students veered between them as they attempted to resolve the problems they encountered in adopting one approach or the other. Moreover, towards the end of the work they described their different approaches tended to converge. For these reasons both patterns have been brought together here and described as depicting a fragmented approach to practice. The two patterns are described in more detail in the following section of this chapter from the perspective of the ways in which the students went about obtaining and interpreting information about the situations they described.

Obtaining and interpreting information

The students' approach to obtaining and interpreting information is examined here under similar headings to those employed in the previous chapter. Their initial approach to the work they described, up to and including their first meetings with the people concerned, is again be examined first. The main themes which emerged from their responses to questions about how their work had proceeded are then drawn out in order to illustrate the two patterns which ensued. Finally, the implications for their understanding of the situations they described are examined.

The initial stages of the students' work

As was seen in the previous chapter, in the context of the everyday social approach the students' treatment of the information available prior to their first meetings with their informants had been limited to what could be gleaned about the potential for establishing the kind of warm relationships they wanted to establish. In contrast, in the context of the fragmented approach the students placed greater emphasis both on interpreting the information available to them in terms of its meaning for the situation to hand, and on identifying lines of enquiry which might be pursued in the course of their first meetings. In interpreting the information to hand and in identifying potentially relevant lines of enquiry they drew on ready made theoretical explanations. This student's response to a question about her initial approach was not untypical:

> There was a lot of information in the file and I went through it several times. I was trying to use some of the things we'd had in the lectures so I was looking for what indications there might be about why he'd started offending at this stage in his life. That gave me some idea of the areas it might be useful to look at in the interview. (First placement student)

Although this approach to the information initially available was echoed by most of the students whose accounts are the focus of this discussion, their aims for their first meetings did not revolve only around the exploration of the lines of enquiry they identified. Rather, their aims had been twofold: to explore those areas they thought relevant on the basis of the theoretical explanations to which they referred, and to establish a helpful relationship with the people concerned. From the students'

51

perspective, however, these aims were not readily compatible because their ideas about the establishment of a helpful relationship remained centred on their everyday knowledge about how successful social interactions are managed, while the exploration of the areas they thought relevant required a more structured approach. In order to resolve this conflict of aims the students drew a distinction between their main aim for their initial meetings with their informants and their secondary aim. It was from the distinction they drew that the two patterns outlined earlier evolved. In those cases where the students deployed theory only with hindsight their main aim had been the establishment of a warm, friendly relationship. These students reported that they had hoped to concentrate on establishing such a relationship in the course of their first meeting, with the intention of introducing a more structured approach later. As this student put it:

> I wanted to kill two birds with one stone, as it were. I wanted to be clear about why I was there, and I knew there were certain areas it might be useful to explore if I could, but I also wanted to present myself as someone who was caring and genuinely concerned, a nice guy if you like. So really, for the first meeting I was prepared to see what happened. If the sort of areas I was interested in came up that was fine, but if not I was happy for it to stay at the level of introductions and getting to know each other a bit. I thought I could always go back later to get more information. (Final placement student)

Amongst those students who placed a similar emphasis on the establishment of a warm relationship several indicated that the dilemmas they faced in delineating their aims for their first meetings had been compounded by their interpretation of the principles of practice to which they aspired. To these students the formulation of ideas and plans seemed tantamount to a judgemental, overly directive approach, as this student explained:

> I did have some ideas at that stage, because in many ways the kind of issues which seemed to be involved were familiar to me from my where I'd worked before. That's something that has worried me a lot on this placement, though. The way things were done in the team was to find out as much as you can first but I can't see how that fits with the non-judgemental attitude we're supposed to have. I wanted to get to know them a bit first rather than getting carried away with too many fancy ideas of my own. (First placement student)

In marked contrast with the hesitancy of this approach, other students indicated that their main aim for their first meeting had been the establishment of a purposeful and business like climate which they had intended to soften later. In their concern to establish this kind of climate, however, their everyday knowledge about how successful social interactions are managed was displaced. This extract provides an illustration:

My main concern at that stage was to make sure I covered all the areas I wanted to cover. I think I had the idea that once I'd got the information I wanted, then I could concentrate on building a relationship with him. (First placement student)

When the students were required to undertake statutory duties the conflict of aims described here was compounded, because from their perspective it was not possible to present themselves both as a concerned, helpful individual and as an official representative of an agency with statutory duties to carry out. As this student put it:

I think a lot of the problems I've had on this placement have been to do with the type of work you get in an area team. Most of the work is statutory work and that's not really the kind of social work I'm interested in. ... It's very difficult I think to convince people you're there to help when actually you're there in an official capacity. (First placement student)

In some cases the students' concerns about undertaking statutory work reinforced their emphasis on establishing a helpful relationship with the people concerned before attempting to introduce a more structured approach, since by doing so they hoped to be able to legitimate the activities they were required to carry out. In other cases, however, a statutory requirement for social work involvement compounded the students' concern to establish a business like climate in the course of their first meeting with the people concerned, since they hoped in this way to imbue their approach with an authority they felt was otherwise lacking.

In response to questions about how their first meetings had worked out, those students whose approach was associated with the hindsight deployment of theory described meetings which were not dissimilar to those associated with the everyday social approach. Although they wanted to be clear about the purpose of their meeting, and had identified some potentially useful lines of enquiry, their primary concern had remained focussed on establishing a warm, harmonious relationship. As a result, their statement of their purpose was typically confined to a brief introduction along the lines of their name, that of the agency they represented and the immediate reason for their visit. Subsequently their initial interactions were not unlike ordinary conversations, in that they followed whatever lines their informants introduced and avoided imposing more structure in the interests of developing a warm relationship. In accordance with their initial plans some of these students left their first meetings without obtaining very much further information. In contrast, those students who entered their initial interactions with the intention of taking a business-like, structured approach found it difficult to establish a helpful climate for their work. As this extract illustrates, in their concern to structure their interactions they found themselves unable to respond to their informants with the warmth and spontaneity they had hoped eventually to achieve:

> I spent far more time planning and preparing for that meeting than I would have before. I was trying to look at it from a family work point of view and I wanted to be very clear about what I was doing. I made a list of all the information I needed to get in my notebook so I could take it in with me. The thing was, although I could plan what I was going to say, I couldn't plan their responses, and that's something that has been a difficulty with other cases too, how to respond to what people say. Before I would have been much more spontaneous about it, but now I feel as if I have to think of the right response - what would a social worker say here, kind of thing. A good example in this case was when her father piped up during that first meeting and said did I know she was a bed wetter. I didn't know what to say. I think I just said something like oh, we don't need to go into all the details just now, but I'll make a note of it, thank you. (First placement student)

This sort of approach was associated with a range of concerns about the presentation of self which contrasted sharply with those associated both with the everyday social approach and with the hindsight deployment of theory. While the concerns associated with those approaches revolved around the students' desire to be perceived as friendly, likeable individuals, in the context of this approach their main concern was to be perceived as proficient social workers. This student's description of her initial contact with her client's family provides an illustration:

> I'd just begun to explain why I was there when his father butted in. He went on and on about the best way to get to the school. I was standing there smiling and nodding politely, but I kept thinking I should be getting back to the point here. I was irritated by it really, this man going on about different routes to the school when I was trying to explain why I was there. ... I was quite shaken by it. I'd been so intent on making a good impression as the new social worker, because first impressions are important I think, and they'd managed to wrap me round their little fingers before I'd even explained why I was there. (First placement student)

A second student made a connection between a similar preoccupation and her concern to use theory in practice:

> If only I'd been able to relax more. I was over anxious I think to put some of the learning from the course into practice, and part of that was this need to impress them, to demonstrate that what I was doing was really work, that I wasn't just sitting chatting idly. (First placement student)

Although the dilemmas described here have been presented as a conflict between different sources of knowledge about acting in the social world, they were not necessarily experienced by the students as clear cut choices about how to approach their work. Rather, from the students' own perspective they appear to have been experienced as an acute and uncomfortable conflict between their role as ordinary, adult members of society and their role as social workers. This role conflict was highlighted by the students' responses to questions about what they felt had helped or might have helped them to resolve the problems they described. In the eyes of many students the answer lay in having a second worker present to carry the more purposeful role which appeared incompatible with the establishment of a helpful relationship. This extract illustrates the kind of solutions they proposed:

I think the only thing that might have helped would have been to have a co-worker, someone who could bring things back to the point when they started getting off it. It's so easy to get side tracked, and it's very hard to get back to the point without seeming rude. (First placement student)

In contrast, other students responded by suggesting that a second worker might have been able to create a helpful climate for their work while they themselves concentrated on structuring their approach. This student in fact responded by describing how she had actually relied on her colleagues to create a helpful climate for their work:

I can probably answer that question best by telling you how I used the other members of the team. I was very aware that I used them to do all the nice nurturing bits, you know, making sure everyone is comfortable and so on. I find it difficult to be as clear as I like to be and at the same time remember all these other bits that are important too. (Beginning student)

Some students described a not dissimilar displacement of one facet of their role in response to questions about what had helped them in carrying out statutory duties. In effect they had sought to legitimate their activities by disowning them, as it were, and displacing them onto the agencies under whose auspices they were working. For example:

I think when you're doing this kind of work you've got to have the attitude that the things you are doing are not necessarily things you think are right, they're things that have to be done. You have to remember that there's a large organisation behind you which sanctions what you're doing. That's where your authority comes from, not from yourself. (Final placement student)

Other students had attempted to reinforce their statutory role by meeting with the people concerned in an office setting. As this student explained, however, this choice of setting could contribute to the rigidity of their approach:

I think part of the problem was working in an office. A few people had said that with statutory work it's often a good idea to meet at the office, especially with teenagers because it gives you some authority. I'm not sure about that now. To me it felt very awkward, the official feel of things. It's very hard to respond naturally to people in that kind of setting. (First placement student)

As was the case with the everyday social approach, the ways in which the students approached the initial stages of their work were both a prelude to and a pattern for the remainder of their work. The main themes which emerged from their accounts in relation to the two patterns which characterised the fragmented approach will be examined here in turn.

The hindsight deployment of theory

Despite their intention of returning to collect information more systematically once they had established the kind of relationship they wanted with the people concerned, those students who deployed theory only with hindsight experienced difficulty in doing so. Instead, they found themselves caught up in the currents and undercurrents of their interactions, struggling to change both the direction and tone of their work. As this student put it:

> It seemed like a good idea to get a bit of a relationship going first and then see where to go from there, but that was more difficult than I thought. It was as if we'd got into this cosy relationship and it was very difficult to change that. It was almost like needing to be two different people, one a chatty, friendly person and the other a more official, social worky type. (First placement student)

The difficulties experienced by these students in changing the direction and tone of their work were associated with a range of problems which revolved around two main themes: the discussion of potentially difficult or embarrassing issues, and perceived conflicts of opinion between themselves and the people with whom they worked. It was seen in the previous chapter that anxieties about addressing subjects which are generally considered taboo in everyday social discourse had played an influential part in shaping the everyday social approach. In the context of an approach involving the hindsight deployment of theory the part played by these anxieties was no less influential, not least because, in the light of the ready made explanations to which they referred, the students were more likely to identify difficult events in their informants' lives, or factors associated with their personal relationships, as potentially relevant lines of enquiry. In effect the taboos which surround the discussion of certain subjects in everyday life appeared to the students to preclude the possibility of discussing some of the issues they thought relevant on the basis of their theoretical knowledge. Their anxieties about raising these issues were therefore a major obstacle to the use of theory in practice. This student's

56

description of the problem he encountered provides an illustration:

> It wasn't difficult to arrive at some sort of idea about why he might be in that situation. The problem was, how I was going to get any confirmation of whether my ideas were in any way accurate. These were very touchy subjects, and I was very dubious about raising that sort of thing with him. (First placement student)

In some cases the students had hoped that the establishment of a warm relationship would enable their informants to raise such issues themselves:

> It was pretty clear, from the information I had, that his relationships with his mother and stepfather, that that was something I needed to explore. The thing was I felt very uncomfortable about raising such personal issues. I had the idea that once we'd established a rapport, maybe in three or four weeks time, then he would raise them himself. But he didn't, so that was wrong as well. (First placement student)

This reluctance to raise difficult issues could be compounded by the students' conceptualisation of the principles of practice to which they aspired, in that they found it difficult to reconcile taking the initiative in raising issues for discussion with the principle of client self determination. Hence, as this extract indicates, they looked to their informants for permission to discuss difficult issues:

> Looking back on it, I wonder if I should maybe have tackled the bereavement issue and the unresolved grief that seemed to be around that more than I did. But after all, she's got a right to decide what should be discussed and what shouldn't, and from the cues I was getting she was backing away from that. I'm still a bit confused about that though, whether I should have been a bit more directive there. (First placement student)

While several students echoed this concern about addressing subjects such as death or sexuality which are commonly considered taboo in the context of everyday social discourse, those students who had undertaken statutory work with children and their families indicated that their most acute anxieties had revolved around raising issues relating to parenting and child care. From their perspective, to raise these issues was to violate the rights of the parents with whom they worked. This student described how concerns of this kind had contributed to the hesitancy of her approach:

> The thing that's worried me most right throughout this placement is how much right you really have to intervene in peoples' lives. I mean ok, this kid has tried to set fire to things and I know you have to do something about that. But this family also have the right to conduct their family life without interference, and the very fact of my involvement was a criticism of the way they were conducting their lives. So how do you resolve that? That's what I want to know. (First placement student)

A second student's description of the difficulties she encountered in raising issues relating to the protection of a child provides an illustration of the ambivalence and hesitancy which could ensue:

> One of the things my supervisor said I needed to raise with them was the fireguard. They'd only put it up while we were there for the baby, they hadn't had it up when the little girl was in the room. ... The first time I went round on my own I was dreading it. I thought supposing they don't have it up, how on earth am I going to say this. ... I suppose it's because they're the parents. There's a feeling of what right do I have to tell these people what to do. ... Of course when I got there they didn't have it up and the little girl was playing right in front of the fire. I kept thinking I'm going to have to say something. Then she started to lean back, right into the fire. It was really dangerous because her hair is quite long and she was leaning right back into the fire. Neither of them reacted at all, they were just sitting there nice and relaxed while I was getting more and more anxious. In the end I leaned forward and kind of put my arm around her shoulders and moved her away. ... I think I said something like 'you really should put the fireguard up', but they didn't take much notice. (Final placement student)

As in the context of the everyday social approach, then, in the context of this approach the students experienced difficulties in undertaking statutory work which revolved around the problem of balancing the needs and interests of those involved. Interwoven with their concern about raising difficult issues for discussion was a second concern which compounded this problem, namely that the development of their own ideas constituted a conflict of opinion with the people concerned. It was seen in the previous chapter that in the context of the everyday social approach conflicts of opinion between the students and the people with whom they worked had not posed problems. The students had, however, spoken of conflicts of opinion between the people with whom they worked and other professionals. These conflicts had arisen when the professionals concerned had interpreted information in ways other than those in which it was presented by the students' informants. Similarly, in the context of this approach when the students themselves interpreted information in ways other than that in which it was presented, that is in terms of the theoretical explanations on which they drew, they regarded this as tantamount to disagreeing with their informant's views. As a result their reluctance to expose their own lines of thought was greatly reinforced, since to do so seemed likely to jeopardise their relationship with the people concerned. Some students felt in addition that by exposing their own ideas they might exacerbate an already difficult or painful situation. For example:

> I was trying to use some of the things we'd had in human development, and from that point of view I was pretty sure her mother's remarriage had a lot to do with it. The problem was what to do with that. It was all very well for me to have all these theories but she wasn't going to see it

like that. And anyway, if it was true I didn't want to rub it in by talking about it all the time. (First placement student)

Other students equated the expression of their own ideas with a judgemental attitude:

I'm not sure I did make sense of it. What I did reach was a way of describing the situation which I felt I could present to my client. My main concern was not to appear overly judgemental. What I did was to describe her situation in very material terms which didn't contradict the things she'd told me. My ideas about why she might be in that situation I kept to myself. (Final placement student)

The way in which some students accounted for the difficulties they experienced in expressing ideas based on the theoretical explanations to which they referred reveal an interesting aspect of the relationship between their use of theory and more everyday sources of understanding. As in the context of the everyday social approach, those students who deployed theory only with hindsight in the context of the fragmented approach placed emphasis on the importance of their affective responses, in addition to their theoretical knowledge, as a source of information about the feelings and needs of the people with whom they worked. When describing their use of these two sources of knowledge they often spoke of resonances between the two. This student, for example, drew a comparison between the concept of scapegoating, which she associated with her education and training, and her own more everyday understanding of group processes:

I'm not sure how different my ideas would have been before the course. I might not have called it scapegoating, that's probably come from the lectures, but I would have known she was being treated unfairly. I mean we've all had experiences of being in groups where that happens. Like at school, there were always kids who got all the stick, I think everyone is aware of that. Even when I was a kid I knew that was unfair, and I think without calling it scapegoating I would have had a lot of sympathy for the position she was in. (First placement student)

In the earlier stages of their education and training some students spoke of the discovery of this sort of resonance between theory and their more everyday knowledge with considerable enthusiasm and excitement. As one student put it: 'I was over the moon! It felt like I really knew something instead of being just a dumb first year'. As they progressed through training, however, unless they were able to overcome the difficulties they experienced in structuring their face to face interactions, the students lost this sense of discovery and excitement. Instead they began to question the value of using theory at all, and they used resonances between theory and their more everyday knowledge in order to legitimate an unstructured, atheoretical approach. This student's response to a question about the way in which she had made sense of the information she obtained provides an illustration:

> I'd have to say it was based more on gut feeling than theory. I know courses have to teach theory, but I'm not sure you need to use theory in practice as much as they say you should. I mean you don't need theories of human development to know that your parents' divorce is a very significant event and I don't see why something is more valid just because someone has written it in a book. I think what the theory does is to tell you when you're on the right lines. Like in this case, it made me more aware of the sort of things that might upset her, so I could be careful to avoid those things, but I don't really think it changed the way I made sense of it. (First placement student)

In some cases the role these students attributed to theory vis a vis their more everyday knowledge was restricted to a way of legitimating an unstructured, atheoretical approach only to those in whose eyes a theoretical account was necessary. As this extract illustrates, this kind of legitimation was most commonly employed in meeting course requirements:

> I know I said in the dissertation that I was using systems theory, but if I'm honest I'd have to say that that was more just to be able to put some theory in. I'm not sure that you really need to refer to theory when you're actually working. It's hard to put a value on it, but I would say that in this case I drew more on my own knowledge of tensions in families and of what it's like to be a disappointment to your family than on any particular theory. It wasn't hard for me to imagine what it was like for her to be in that situation. I mean that might be developed by the lectures on family work, but I don't think you necessarily need that kind of explicit framework. There are some very common sense understandings of these things. (Final placement student)

The accounts in question indicate that this kind of legitimation of an unstructured, atheoretical approach was part of a vicious circle in which the students became enmeshed. On the one hand, they were able to account for their difficulties in structuring their interactions by questioning the need to make use of theory in practice. On the other hand, those same difficulties, which have been seen to stem from a conflict between the norms and conventions of social discourse and the introduction of a more structured approach, also prevented them from making their more everyday understandings explicit. Hence, as in the context of the everyday social approach, their affective responses remained at the level of unchecked assumptions about the feelings and needs of the people with whom they worked. A second extract from the account quoted above provides an illustration:

> **J.S.** Was that something you discussed at all with her, the tensions in her own family?

Student No, we never directly discussed it, though it was there in the background. There was never any opportunity to discuss it actually. She didn't bring it up herself, and I was dubious about getting into that kind of area unless she raised it herself. It's only speculation, but my hunch would be that there were some pretty sensitive issues there, and I was very wary of raising those issues with her.

When the students attempted to deploy ready made theory as recipes for practice the problems they experienced were quite different from those which have been described here. The main themes which emerged from their accounts are contrasted below with those associated with the hindsight deployment of theory.

The deployment of theory as recipes for practice

When the students persisted in deploying theory as recipes for practice they continued to experience difficulty in creating a helpful climate for their work. In effect, their capacity to elicit and explore the views of the people with whom they worked was impeded by their concern with purpose and structure. Moreover, in contrast with the hesitancy expressed by other students about pre-judging a situation or being overly directive, these students found themselves neglecting the principles of practice to which they aspired. This student's response to a question about how her meetings with her client had worked out provides an illustration:

> I'm so embarrassed about it now. I had the idea that if I started off very structured I would be able to relax a bit more later. It didn't work out like that though. That first meeting was the pattern, really, for several meetings. I'd go through my notes of the last one and draw up an agenda for the next one. I'm so ashamed of myself. It wasn't until about half way through the placement that I realised I was so concerned with what I wanted to do that I hadn't left any room to find out what he might want. (First placement student)

In some cases the students were so dismayed at the results of their attempts to make use of theory in practice that they abandoned this approach and veered towards the pattern associated with the hindsight deployment of theory. Other students, however, redoubled their efforts. They attributed their failure to manage their interactions successfully to insufficient planning and returned to subsequent meetings with the aim of exerting greater control over their format and content. For example:

> I got very disheartened with it all. No matter what I did I couldn't seem to get any control in the interviews. I had a look at some of the literature on family work but all the books seem to assume that people want to work with you. They don't tell you what to do when all you get is grunts and monosyllabic answers. The idea of circular questioning was something I thought I could try though. I decided to use that the

next time I saw them, so I sat down and wrote out a list of about forty questions to ask. ... I'm not sure how well it worked. A lot of the time they just answered in monosyllables. It felt a bit like an interrogation. I was pleased that I'd managed to get through everything I wanted to ask, because at least I'd managed to get some control of it, and I think they did respect me a bit more after that. But when I looked at my notes afterwards, I didn't really get much information from them. (First placement student)

Like this student, other students who attempted to deploy theory as recipes for practice reported that their approach had resulted in an interrogatory feel to their interactions which contrasted sharply with the concern associated with a more everyday approach that information should emerge as though from ordinary conversation. They often said that they had felt rigid or robotic, as though playing an unaccustomed role. Some students highlighted this sense of inauthenticity by referring to a more everyday, conversational approach as one of 'being myself'. The student quoted above, for example, describing her next meeting with her client's family, added as an aside that she had 'stopped circular questioning by then' and was 'being more myself'.

As has been seen, when the students deployed theory only with hindsight, the problems they experienced in raising issues for discussion had contributed to the hesitancy of their approach. In the context of this approach the problems associated with raising issues for discussion were rather different. Here, the students' concerns did not revolve around the legitimacy of raising issues they thought relevant, because from their perspective the exploration of lines of enquiry formulated on the basis of a theoretical explanation provided sufficient legitimation for doing so. Hence, not only was their everyday knowledge about the management of interactions displaced by their use of ready made theory, but the potential for conflicts of opinion was also glossed over. This students' assessment of her approach provides an illustration:

As I said earlier, I was over anxious to put some of the learning from the course into practice, and in that sense it was a very head thing. There wasn't a lot of feeling. It seems so obvious now, but at the time it was as if I forgot to put myself, even for a minute, in their shoes, especially Stuart himself. I think that's why I let myself rush in with my airy fairy notions when I had been so determined to be calm and considered about it. If only I'd taken a bit of time to get to know him better, to look at it through his eyes a bit more. That's something I've struggled with in more than one case, how you can use theory, which I think is important, without forgetting the feelings side of things. (First placement student)

Although it is not possible to know with any certainty how the students' approach to raising issues they thought relevant was perceived, from their own perspective the people with whom they worked rarely responded as they expected to their overtures. For example:

Student I was trying to look at it in terms of some of the things we'd had in the human development lectures, and I mean when you looked at it like that he'd had so many losses in his life. I felt sure the way he was in hospital was connected with that, so for me that suggested that some kind of counselling was what was required. The trouble was, he just wasn't able to respond to that. He wasn't interested in talking about his past.

J.S. How did you approach it with him, can you remember?

Student Well, I don't think I put it quite as directly as that. I may have said something like perhaps if we look at some of the things that have happened in the past, that might help. I just assumed that if we could talk about those things, then he would gain some sort of insight. (First placement student)

When the people with whom they worked did respond to their overtures, further problems ensued from the rigidity of the students' approach. This student's description of the problems she encountered was one which was echoed by several other students:

It all seemed very clear in the books. The problem was, how do you put that into practice? The literature was helpful as far as it went, but it's what you do when someone starts telling you all these terribly painful things. I seemed to freeze up at that point. I was so worried about saying the wrong thing that I didn't know what to say, and nobody seemed able to tell me. (Beginning student)

The problems encountered by the students in obtaining and interpreting information were reflected in their responses to questions about their eventual understanding of the situations they described. These responses are examined next, before moving on to the final section of the chapter.

The students' understanding of the situations they described

It will be clear from the preceding discussion that in the context of this approach the students' understanding of the situations they described were not couched only in the terms in which information was obtained. Instead, regardless of which pattern their work followed, in responding to questions about their eventual understanding they referred to the theoretical explanations on which they had drawn in interpreting information. As in the context of the everyday social approach, however, the students experienced difficulty in arriving at an overall understanding of the situations they described. The problems associated with the two patterns which have been described here will be considered in turn.

The hindsight deployment of theory In the context of an approach involving the hindsight deployment of theory the students were only able to focus on making sense of the information they obtained in the light of the theoretical explanations to which they referred once they were removed from the pressures of their face to face interactions. When face to face with the people with whom they worked their approach was not dissimilar to that described in the previous chapter, in that they accepted the information offered as facts of the case which required no further exploration. This student's description of the problems she encountered provides an illustration:

> That's something that worries me a bit, that I'm not able to think about things as they're happening. When I'm with my clients I feel a bit like a sponge: I'm soaking it all in but I can't do anything with it. I sit there nodding and smiling and trying to look sympathetic but inside it's a panicky feeling - what on earth does all this mean kind of thing. It's only when I'm on the bus or back in the office that I can really think about what they were saying and all the other things that were going on. That's where the theory comes in, but I can't seem to use it at the time. It's still based on gut reaction rather than theory. (First placement student)

As in the context of the everyday social approach the problems experienced by the students in making sense of the information they obtained were compounded when they worked with groups of people, and particularly when they encountered differences of opinion amongst the people concerned. Rather than taking sides, however, in the context of this approach the students drew on their theoretical knowledge in an attempt to make sense of the conflicts they encountered. Again, though, they were only able to do so after the event. When face to face with the people with whom they worked they remained unsure about how to respond. As a result their role was usually that of a silent, uncomfortable observer. Once removed from the immediacy of their face to face interactions, however, they were able to begin to make sense of the conflicts they had witnessed, albeit too late to guide their own response. This student described both his immediate response to a family dispute, and the way in which he had later made sense of that dispute:

> I'm aware that I find that very difficult, when people are arguing, and this instance was fairly typical. It was like being paralysed. I just left in the end. I think I said something ineffectual like perhaps we can talk about this again next week. Later, once I'd got back to the office, I could see it wasn't as catastrophic as it had felt. In many ways I learnt more about the family from that argument than from all the other meetings. I could see lots of things it might have been useful to follow up. So that was a missed opportunity, a chance to strike while the iron was hot that I completely missed. (First placement student)

Although these students were able, then, to reflect after the event on the information they obtained, they remained unable to explore the lines of thought which emerged in the course of their face to face interactions, because to do so conflicted with their ideas about the maintenance of a helpful relationship. Instead, when face to face with their informants they continued to absorb information as events unfolded, while giving little or no indication of the direction their own thoughts were taking. As a result, their accounts of their eventual understanding of the situations they described had a tentative, almost ruminative tone about them. In contrast with the everyday social approach, they did not present their informants' views as straightforward facts of the case. Rather, they supplemented those views with their own speculative lines of thought for which they could present some argument but little confirmation. As in the previous chapter, it is difficult to illustrate the students responses to questions about their eventual understanding without including long, unwieldy extracts from their accounts. Here again, however, their responses to questions about their written work provide some indication of the problems they encountered. This response was fairly typical:

> I'm not sure that writing case notes was much help really. For one thing, I was aware that other people would be reading them, and I didn't want to make too many judgements. So much of my thinking about the case was no more than that, my own opinions, and I was very wary of putting that on paper. I tended just to put down the obvious things, facts about the family and the things that happened. The trouble was so much happened that it was hard to know where to start. I tended to write far too much I think, just to get everything down. (Final placement student)

The deployment of theory as recipes for practice   When the students attempted to deploy theory as recipes for practice, their responses to questions about their eventual understanding of the situations they described were rather different. As has been seen, the majority of students who took this approach had interpreted the information they obtained in terms of ready made theoretical explanations acquired in the course of their education and training. In contrast with other students, however, they had taken the validity of this ready made knowledge for granted. From their perspective, explanations derived from different theoretical frameworks were applicable in rule book fashion to different kinds of situation. Where work with children and families was concerned a systemic explanation was regarded as the explanation of choice and other explanations were ruled out. On the other hand, where work with an individual was concerned this kind of explanation was considered inappropriate and a psychodynamic explanation was usually chosen. Thus the students' choice of explanation was influenced more by the configuration of people with whom they worked than by an analysis of their situation per se. In a few cases, however, their choice of explanation was made not on this basis, but because a particular way of thinking about situations was familiar to them from previous experiences of practice. In these cases the students had assumed that their familiar approach to making sense of a situation was appropriate for the new situations they encountered in the course of their education and training.

Whatever the basis of their choice of explanation, the students' approach to making sense of information was not very different in many respects from that associated with the everyday social approach, despite considerable differences in the content of the knowledge on which they drew. While they did not take the information they obtained at face value as straightforward facts of the case, there was nevertheless a taken for granted quality about their approach, in that they immediately assimilated the information they obtained to their own pre-selected explanations. From that point on these explanations were taken for granted as facts of the case which required no further exploration. Instead of exploring or seeking confirmation of the validity of their ideas, the students proceeded straight away to implement the kind of intervention which seemed, rule book fashion, to fit. Consequently, as in the context of other approaches, their ideas remained at the level of unchecked assumptions.

Because this pattern was closely associated with the ways in which the students attempted to help the people with whom they worked it will be explored more fully in the final section of this chapter. Of interest here, however, is the fact that in common with other students these students experienced difficulty in arriving at an overall understanding of the situations they described, in this case because the interventions they attempted did not meet with the expected results. Having failed to achieve the expected results the students decided that their initial choice of theoretical explanation was untenable and quickly replaced it with another recipe like formula. Whatever their second choice, however, they rarely met with success in achieving the results they expected, and eventually fell back on more everyday explanations of the situations they described. The processes involved will be explored more fully shortly. In the meantime this extract offers an indication of the implications for the students' ability to arrive at an understanding of the situations they described:

A lot of the work I've done on this placement has been with families and children, and my practice teacher is very keen on systems theory so I've been trying to use that a lot. The trouble is, it isn't always that useful. By the third meeting, I was sure that a lot of the little girl's behaviour was functional, though I still didn't know what the dynamics were. It stayed at that level for a long time, and I still don't think I've got the measure of them. I gave up on systems theory because they just couldn't see it that way. I thought a more task centred approach might work better, though I was still convinced her behaviour was functional. But there again they didn't do the things they were supposed to. I found it very difficult to make any sense of what was going on. In the end, what I felt was that they needed a granny, someone to be around and help with the hassle of being adults and parents. (Final placement student)

The different problems encountered by these students in making use of theory in practice were associated with accounts of their eventual understanding which were constructed differently from those associated with the hindsight deployment of theory. In place of the tentative, ruminative accounts associated with that approach, in the context of this approach the students' accounts had an episodic, disjointed quality. An illustration is provided by their response to the story like framework of the research interview schedule, in that they found it difficult to think of their work in terms of a beginning, middle and end. From their perspective their work seemed to have a multitude of beginnings, as one theory was replaced by another. As one student put it: 'It's difficult to say when the work really began. I always seemed to be beginning and never getting anywhere.' Again the students' responses to questions about their written work reflect the problems they encountered in arriving at a more cohesive understanding. This student's description of her case notes was not untypical:

The case notes? Do I have to be honest? I'm pretty ashamed of them now. I started off alright, as I thought, with nice clear headings about assessment, goals and interventions, but as it went on they just dissolved into a mess. There were lots of times I wished I could tear them up and start again. It was very hard to keep up with what was happening and none of my fancy ideas ever came to much. The worst part about it was when it came to writing a summary. I thought where on earth do I start with this lot. (First placement student)

As in the context of the everyday social approach, the ways in which the students attempted to help the people with whom they worked were closely interwoven with the ways in which they obtained and interpreted information. This aspect of their work is now considered in the final section of the chapter.

Helping people in the context of the fragmented approach

In order to explore the ways in which the students attempted to help the people with whom they worked in the context of the fragmented approach, the following discussion will focus on the fifteen accounts of practice which were most typical of the approach. As will be seen in the following chapter, when the students were able to resolve some of the conflicts and dilemmas described here a different pattern emerged. Amongst the fifteen accounts which will be considered nine were typical of the hindsight deployment of theory, while six were typical of the deployment of theory as recipes for practice. The different approaches to helping people associated with each of these patterns will be considered in turn.

When the students deployed theory only with hindsight in the context of the fragmented approach the ways in which they attempted to help the people with whom they worked were not dissimilar in some respects to those associated with the everyday social approach. Here too, as a result of their reluctance to introduce their own lines of enquiry and thought, they were dependent to a large extent on the ideas and initiatives of the people with whom they worked. Underlying this similarity, however, were some rather different themes which will be examined here.

In three cases the students whose accounts are the focus of this discussion experienced considerable problems because they were unable to establish the kind of relationship they wanted with the people with whom they worked. Under these circumstances, their efforts were centred on endeavouring to establish a relationship rather than on more directly attempting to help the people concerned. While their inability to establish the kind of relationship they wanted may have been the result of variables not addressed by the research, for example the background characteristics of the people involved or unknown factors associated with their particular situations, the students' accounts suggest that it was associated to some extent at least with the ambivalence of their own approach. Although they wanted to establish the kind of warm, friendly relationships associated with the everyday social approach, these students appear to have been unable to approach the people with whom they worked in an unequivocally warm, friendly way because, as has been seen, this kind of approach was perceived to conflict with their secondary aim of adopting a more structured way of working. As this extract from one of the accounts in question illustrates, the relationships they did describe reflected their ambivalence:

> The most difficult thing was the frustration I think. I'd pinned all my hopes on being able to get a good relationship with her, especially because that was something the field social worker hadn't been able to do, but it didn't work out. ... I think it was just because it was a very difficult role. I wanted to be a friend to her, someone she could come and talk to, but at the same time I was her key worker and I needed to be able to work with her on that level too. Maybe it's possible to get some sort of balance, but I didn't manage it. I was worried that she would see me as too friendly and easy going, but I didn't want to bore her either by always talking about heavy things. (First placement student)

Faced with their inability to establish the kind of relationship they wanted, both this student and another student eventually gave up on their attempt to do so, and hence on their attempt to help. This extract from the account of the second student provides an illustration:

> One of the things was the worry about not having much to offer in terms of shared interests or common ground. I think if I could start

again I would wrack my brains for something we could do together. I think perhaps there was a lack of confidence that we could enjoy something together or make progress in that way. There was a dread of planning enjoyment when so much of it depends on spontaneity. I suppose in the end I didn't want to really. That's what it boils down to. (First placement student)

Although the third student's experience was rather different his account lends support to the idea that the ambivalence of the students' approach had contributed to the problems they described. In this case, rather than abandoning his attempt to establish the kind of relationship he wanted, and hence his attempt to help, the student abandoned his secondary aim of adopting a more structured way of working in favour of a more everyday approach. In doing so he found that he was able to establish the kind of relationship he wanted with his client, and that his client was subsequently able to identify and address some concerns:

One of the biggest problems with this case was that he was hardly ever there for our appointments, and when he was he was uncommunicative to say the least. After he went missing from the home for the third time I thought I'm not carrying on like this. It felt dishonest, all this investigating and theorising behind his back. I decided for the rest of the placement that I was just going to be a friend to him, and that's what I did. We went out for a pint or a coffee and enjoyed ourselves. It was during one of those outings that he finally told me where he'd been going. After that things improved a great deal. He began to talk about some of the things that were concerning him, and he began to suggest other things we could do in our time together, like finding his wife's grave. That was something that had been on his mind. (First placement student)

There are, then, some indications here that the students' conflicting aims in approaching their work in some cases diminished their capacity to offer the kind of warm, friendly relationship they wanted to offer, and hence their ability to help the people with whom they worked.

In three of the remaining six cases under consideration the people with whom the students worked had identified some specific needs or problems, but had been unsuccessful in addressing them. Under these circumstances, as in the context of the everyday social approach, the students were also at a loss as to how to help, in this case because the kind of interventions which seemed appropriate on the basis of their own lines of thought appeared to conflict both with their informant's views, and with their own ideas about the creation of a helpful climate for their work. In the context of this approach, however, the students' approach was different from that described in the previous chapter, in that they neither withdrew from their attempt to help, nor responded in the way a friend or family member might respond. Instead they continued to meet with the people concerned on a regular, planned basis. In the course of their meetings they encouraged them to talk about how things had been between meetings and offered sympathy and general support in times of crisis. At the same time, once removed from the pressures of their face to face interactions, they struggled to obtain an understanding of the situation within which they were working. In the absence of any information about the views of the people with whom the students worked it is not possible to draw any conclusions about the extent to which their persistence and concern was perceived to be helpful. From the students' perspective, however, their time and effort had resulted in little or no change, and although they hoped their involvement might have made some less visible difference, they also expressed frustration and concern about their inability to offer any more concrete help. For example:

I only saw them for an hour or two at the most each week, but I worried about them twenty four hours a day. I even dreamt about them. I always had the feeling I wasn't doing enough and yet there didn't seem to be anything else I could do. (First placement student)

In the remaining three cases the students' approach differed from those described so far, in that they themselves had proposed ways of addressing needs or problems identified by the people with whom they worked. In all three cases, however, the students expressed some dissatisfaction with the ideas they put forward. In two cases their dissatisfaction stemmed from their feeling that their ideas were only stop gap measures which, though apparently successful in the short term, did not address what they themselves saw as the most important issues. In both cases the students indicated that their ideas had been based less on their theoretical knowledge than on more everyday sources of knowledge, which they had later reframed in the terminology of a task centred approach, in much the same way as theoretical explanations were used to legitimate an unstructured approach to obtaining and interpreting information. This student's response to a question about how her work had ended up provides an illustration:

I don't know if it was because it was getting near the end of the placement and I thought I had to do something before I left, but anyway I had the idea in that meeting of asking them to think of something the other one could do which might make things better for them. Her mother said the only thing she wanted was for Tracey to go to school every day, and I thought this is us back where we started. But then Tracey said she would go to school if her mother kept her supplied with cigarettes. That was what she wanted. For the essay I said it was a task centred approach, but it was more like bribery really. It's the sort of thing I've seen my sister do to get my wee nephew to do things he doesn't want to do. Amazingly, so far it seems to have worked. Last time I went round she'd been to school every day for a week. I can't see it lasting though. I'm pretty sure there's a lot more going on in the family, especially between her and the step-father. There's a lot of things in that relationship which make me wonder about sexual abuse, but that's something I don't think I could possibly have tackled. I just hope the next worker will be more able to look at that than I was. (First placement student)

In the third case the student concerned had been able to negotiate child care provision for his client, and he was pleased to have been able to help in this way. He remained dissatisfied, however, with a second idea he had proposed. In this case his dissatisfaction stemmed from his subsequent realisation that this idea in fact conflicted with his own lines of thought:

I was really pleased when the children's centre offered her a place. At least I'd done something useful for her there. It was only for a few hours each day though, so there was still the question of some support in the evenings and at weekends. The natural solution seemed to be for the grandparents to have her when her mum couldn't cope, and my client didn't raise any objections. In some ways though I'm a bit dubious. I mean I don't think this young woman is in the situation she's in for no reason at all, and from what I've seen of her relationship with her parents I could build up quite a list of indications that she may have been sexually abused by her father. On the other hand, if sexual abuse was a problem, no-one was saying so. All the same I was worried about encouraging her to leave the little girl with them. I wonder now if I shouldn't have explored that more, though having said that I'm not at all sure I could have. (Final placement student)

The deployment of theory as recipes for practice

In comparison with the variety of approaches associated with the hindsight deployment of theory, when the students deployed theory as recipes for practice their approach to helping the people with whom they worked was very much more uniform. From the six accounts which were most typical of this approach a strikingly similar pattern emerged which was closely interwoven with the process of interpreting information described earlier. There it was seen that in the majority of cases the students took for granted the validity of ready made theories derived mainly from lectures or textbooks and proceeded directly to implement the kind of interventions which seemed, rule book fashion, to fit. From the perspective of these students, then, the use of a particular theoretical explanation in interpreting information appeared to dictate the kind of help required. As a result their choice of intervention was made not on the basis of an analysis of a particular situation, but on a generic equation of certain situations with particular theories and the methods of intervention associated with them. Thus, where their meetings took place with an individual, and a psychodynamic explanation was the explanation of choice, the deployment of that explanation appeared to the students to require the exploration of past events in the lives of the people with whom they worked and the

71

subsequent acquisition of insight into the present significance of those events on the part of the people concerned. Similarly, when they worked with children and their families the deployment of a systemic perspective appeared to require the cooperation and presence of all family members in order that their inter-relationships might be explored and changes in family functioning engineered. In a few cases, as was seen earlier, the students' choice of explanation had been made not so much on the basis of this rule book approach as on the basis of their familiarity with a particular way of thinking about situations. Hence in these cases their choice of intervention was also made on the basis of their familiarity with particular ways of working.

Clearly, in comparison with other students these students were very much less dependent on the ideas and initiatives of the people with whom they worked. They were, however, dependent instead on the motivation and ability of the people concerned to cooperate, with a minimum of explanation, in the kind of interventions which seemed, recipe fashion, to fit their situation. Although it is not possible to know how the students' attempts at intervention were perceived, from their own perspective the people with whom they worked had, without exception, been either unable or unwilling to cooperate in their first choice of intervention. In these circumstances, as was noted earlier, the students quickly abandoned both their first choice of theory and the type of intervention with which it was associated. At this stage, the accounts of those students who had deployed a particular theory on the basis of its familiarity converged with those of other students. This student, for example, explained why she had abandoned her familiar way of working:

> For a while I got very stuck. Right from my time as a volunteer and in all the jobs I've had that's been the approach, that you try and help people gain insight by helping them to talk things through. But I couldn't get anywhere with that approach because he just wasn't interested in talking about the past. (First placement student)

In the context of family work some students came up against problems because they were unable to secure the participation of all those whose presence they felt was necessary for the deployment of a systemic perspective. This extract provides an illustration:

> I was convinced that the problems didn't begin and end with this child's behaviour. I was pretty clear about that. Where it got less clear was what to do about that. I wanted to look at it with them in a systemic sort of way, but after that first meeting her dad was never in, though I kept stressing that it was really important for them all to be there. There wasn't much point in keeping going with it if he wasn't going to be there. (First placement student)

Other students who attempted to deploy a systemic perspective had been able to secure the presence of all those they thought should be involved, but had nevertheless found themselves unable to pursue the sort of intervention they thought appropriate because the people concerned seemed unwilling or unable to share their perspective. For example:

I'd been trying to use a systemic kind of approach, because I thought if I focussed on the little girl's behaviour that would feed into what they were doing. The trouble was they didn't see it that way at all. They kept bringing everything back to her behaviour so in the end I just gave up. (Final placement student)

Having failed to achieve the results they expected with their first choice of intervention, the students turned to other methods. Their second choice of intervention was often described as a task centred approach, although they rarely referred to the behaviourist ideas which underpin that approach. Instead, the techniques associated with the approach were implemented rule book fashion, on the assumption that the desired results would ensue. It was for this reason that behaviourist ideas were described at the beginning of this chapter as implicit in some students work. In deploying a task centred approach, the students unquestioningly accepted their informants' definitions of the problems they confronted and translated those problems directly into goals, contracts and associated tasks. With one exception, however, the expected results again failed to ensue. Although it is not possible to be certain why this was so, the students' accounts suggest that their approach left little space for any exploration of the complexities of some of the situations they encountered, and particularly of the different perspectives which might be held by those involved. This extract provides an illustration:

Although my own inclination is towards a more therapeutic approach, there was no way they were going to be able to make use of that. I decided what I needed to do was to get back to something very simple and clear, and the task centred approach seemed ideal for that. His mother was very clear about what the problems were, so it seemed fairly straightforward to turn those things into tasks they could work on over the next week or so. She was happy with that, and I was pleased that I seemed to have found a way through the impasse I'd got myself into. When I went back next week though nothing had changed. If anything he was even more withdrawn and his mother was even more frustrated. It seems obvious to me now, what I'd done was to completely miss out his point of view. I mean I can see how to him it must have felt like more of the same, only now there was another person nagging at him. (First placement student)

In the one case where an attempt to deploy a task centred approach had achieved the expected results the question of different perspectives had not arisen, because the student's intervention had involved only her client himself. At a later stage in her work, however, the same student attempted to use the approach again in a context where different perspectives were involved, and her second attempt met with little success:

> I think I assumed that because it worked once, it would work again. It was like having a magic formula: you set goals, make a contract, and hey presto! When it didn't work I was completely thrown. It wasn't until I sat down to write the essay that I was able to look at that more closely. I think what I'd done was I hadn't taken into account the fact that they might all have different goals. I assumed that because they agreed at the meeting, that meant they really agreed. I think now I could have spent a lot more time looking at what they were wanting to change and what they were getting out of things staying the same. It was a lot less straightforward than I imagined. (First placement student)

In the context of work with children and their families the second choice of intervention made by two students was to work individually with different family members. In both cases the students' decision had been prompted by conflicts of opinion amongst family members. One student had responded by attempting to give equal support to those involved. As this extract illustrates, however, this approach led to new dilemmas about how to help:

> I left that meeting feeling absolutely shattered. I felt like I'd been pushed and pulled apart for two hours. I mean here were two women, mother and daughter, who both needed my support to cope with this crisis, yet by supporting one I would be undermining the other. ... The way I dealt with that was by trying to give them both some support. I was literally taking it in turns - supporting the mum over one thing, and then the daughter over another. It was after that meeting that I decided I couldn't see them together any more, so for the rest of the time I saw one one week and one the next. The thing that puzzles me though is how you choose between different theories when you're working with a family like this. There were so many different points of view, depending who you spoke to, and as many different theories to match. I mean you've got bereavement theory, family theory, individual life stages theory, theories of adolescence, and they were all relevant to this one family. Now, how do you integrate that? I wanted to be able to put them together in one picture, but you need an overview for that. (Final placement student)

As a second extract from the same account illustrates, the student concerned began to feel increasingly enmeshed in the situation she described and decreasingly able to help:

> I ended up feeling very much in the middle of it, and I think I was. I was being pushed and pulled, trying to meet all these different needs. I ended up jumping from one theory to another and getting nowhere with any of it. I needed to find a way of planning or organising the data in a way that I could understand it so I could get ahead of the things that were happening, rather than just following on, picking up the pieces.

The second student's response to conflict amongst family members was reminiscent of the everyday social approach, in that she had chosen to work only with the family member who seemed best disposed towards her:

The reason I started seeing his mother on her own was I think because I was a bit frightened of his father. I would have liked to have kept seeing them all together, but I suppose it was a way of allaying my anxiety a bit that I could work with somebody who I knew wouldn't shout at me. At least she could be worked on because she seemed to concede that there were things that were worrying her, whereas he was saying there wasn't a problem and he seemed the sort of person who'd get quite aggressive if you contradicted him. (First placement student)

Eventually, in some cases after trying to implement a third method of intervention, all six students whose accounts are the focus of this discussion exhausted their repertoire and fell back on more everyday explanations of the situations they encountered, including in two cases the use of negative value judgements to explain the failure of their attempts at intervention. In these circumstances, as the following extracts illustrate, the students eventually withdrew from their attempt to help:

In the end it became clear that nothing I did was going to make any difference. I don't want to sound as if I'm making excuses, but I think that had a lot to do with the way this kid was. I mean I like to approach things generally with the attitude that everyone has some strengths, but honestly this kid was so dozy. A more unprepossessing kid it would be difficult to imagine. I suppose that's really why I started seeing them less often, because from my point of view it was very hard work spending an hour with him. (First placement student)

And:

The systems theory didn't really help in the end. I think if I made any sense of it at all I just saw it all individually. He was so surly and unresponsive it was difficult to get anywhere with him, and his father was like that too. He was an aggressive, evasive man. His mother, although she was more amenable to working with me, she didn't make any effort to change anything. I think she was just manipulating me with her cups of tea and kitkats. It got to the stage where I dreaded going round there. I used to put it off as long as I could. (First placement student)

In the remaining four cases the students' failure to achieve the results they expected lead eventually to a pattern identical to that described by some students who had deployed theory only with hindsight, in that they continued to meet with the people concerned on a regular, planned basis without any clear idea about how to help. This extract provides an illustration:

Like I said, eventually I came down to the idea that what they needed was a granny figure to help them cope. Even though it's not a social work role, in the end there wasn't much else I could do. I just hoped that by visiting every week I was doing some good by letting them off load onto me a bit. (Final placement student)

Amongst both these students and those who had ended up in a similar position through deploying theory with hindsight there was a common tendency, in line with the process of legitimation described earlier, to reframe this kind of approach in terms of the kind of methods of intervention associated with a psychodynamic perspective. The student quoted above, for example, added this comment to her description of her eventual approach:

I suppose you could call it more of a therapeutic approach, you know giving people opportunities to ventilate feelings, though I wasn't really thinking of that at the time.

As was noted at the beginning of this chapter, references to the ideas associated with psychodynamic explanations of human development and behaviour featured frequently in the students' accounts. In many cases, however, these references occurred in the context of the kind of reframing documented above. This suggests, then, that the psychodynamic perspective was not necessarily a particularly favoured perspective, although it occurred frequently in the students' accounts. Rather, the everyday activities on which the students eventually fell back were more readily reframed in terms of the 'talking therapies' associated with this perspective than in terms of the other perspectives to which they referred in the course of their accounts.

Before going on to explore the third approach to practice identified in the course of the research the main features of the fragmented approach are summarised below.

Summary

In contrast with the approach described in the previous chapter, in the context of the fragmented approach the students had drawn on the kind of knowledge which is commonly described as theoretical to explain the situations they described. The type of theory on which they drew has been defined as ready made theory because it consisted of explanations which were handed on to the students by teachers and authors or through practice agencies. In making use of this theoretical knowledge the students experienced considerable problems which have been seen to stem from a conflictual relationship between the use of ready made theory and other sources of knowledge. In order to resolve dilemmas stemming from the conflicts they encountered, some students adopted an approach to practice within which they managed their interactions in line with their everyday knowledge and the principles of practice to which they aspired. Consequently they made use of their theoretical knowledge only with hindsight. In contrast, other students took the opposite course and deployed ready made theories as prescriptive recipes for practice which displaced both their everyday knowledge about the management of interactions and the principles of practice to which they aspired.

In the context of the fragmented approach the students continued to experience difficulty in arriving at an understanding of the situations they described. When they deployed theory only with hindsight their hesitancy in exploring lines of thought based on theoretical explanations led to the development of speculative ideas for which no confirmation was sought or obtained. On the other hand, when the students deployed ready made theory as recipes for practice their understanding of the situations they described was fragmented and disjointed, reflecting their abandonment of one theory and method of intervention after another as they failed to achieve the expected results.

Equally, the students experienced difficulty in helping the people with whom they worked. When they had deployed theory only with hindsight some students had been unable to establish the kind of relationship they wanted with the people concerned. In other cases they had been dependent to a large extent on the ideas and initiatives of the people with whom they worked. In those cases where they did make suggestions intended to help the people concerned they remained dissatisfied with the results because their suggestions were not consonant with their own ideas. On the other hand, when they deployed theory as recipes for practice the students had relied on the people with whom they worked cooperating in the interventions they attempted. They very rarely received that cooperation, however, and their interventions rarely met with the expected results.

6 The fluent approach

An overview of the approach

The approach to practice which is the focus of this chapter was distinguished from the fragmented approach on the basis of the ways in which the students used the sort of explanations which are commonly termed theoretical in making sense of the situations they described. As was noted in the previous chapter, in terms of the content of the students' knowledge there was some considerable overlap between the fluent approach to practice and the fragmented approach. In the context of this third approach the students referred to a similar range of theoretical explanations to those described in the previous chapter. There were, however, significant differences in the ways in which they deployed their theoretical knowledge. The main difference lay in the fact that in the context of this approach the students did not rely on ready made theoretical explanations in the form in which they were handed on by teachers and others to make sense of the situations they described. Instead they made use of this ready made knowledge in constructing their own theories. These theories can be described as 'custom made' in order to distinguish them from the ready made theories associated with the fragmented approach. The students' ability to construct custom made theories was associated with the development of a range of cognitive and interpersonal skills which were the hallmark of the fluent approach. The remainder of this preliminary discussion will therefore focus on describing these skills.

Amongst the range of skills which distinguished the fluent approach from the other approaches to practice identified in the course of the research was a skill which perhaps sounds deceptively simple, namely an ability to actively listen in the course of face to face interactions. Within the literature of social work practice the ability to listen appears to be a skill which is largely taken for granted. Davies (1985), for example, does not include this ability amongst the essential skills he describes. Nor is an ability to listen included amongst the core skills required for the award of the new Diploma in Social Work (CCETSW, 1989a). Although Butler and Elliot (1985) include listening in a check list of skills required for practice, in the course of their discussion of these skills talking rather than listening appears to be given precedence:

> In turn, of course, the practitioner needs to work on receiving messages from other people as accurately as possible. This means being prepared to translate, rephrase, and reflect on written, spoken and gestured material ... .(p.26)

Where more attention is paid to listening, the ability appears to be associated only with counselling as a method of intervention. Coulshed (1988, p.26), for example, includes an ability to 'Let a person finish talking without reacting' in her inventory of counselling skills, but makes no mention of this ability in her earlier discussion of assessment skills.

The accounts of the students who took part in this research suggest that this apparent neglect or marginalisation of the ability to listen is misplaced, not least because it was an ability which they experienced particular difficulty in acquiring. Amongst those students who had learnt how to listen by the end of training the development of the ability was regarded as a significant contribution to their practice. As one student put it:

> I no longer feel I have to do something all the time. I can sit and be quiet and just listen. If I've been able to be helpful it's been that rather than any wonderful intervention. (Final placement student)

As this extract from her account suggests, during her first placement this student's approach had been very typical of the deployment of theory as recipes for practice. While it is probably clear that in the context of that approach the students' anxiety to be seen to be proficient intruded on their ability to listen to the people with whom they worked, it might be thought that an ability to listen was a central feature of both the everyday social approach and the hindsight deployment of theory. The students' accounts suggest, however, that there was a qualitative difference between the ways in which they listened in the context of those approaches and the fluent approach. As has been seen, in the context of the everyday social approach the students unquestioningly accepted the information offered by the people with whom they worked. In some cases their approach seems to have been more akin to what Nelson-Jones (1988, p.13) has described as 'hearing' than to listening. In other cases their reliance on affective sources of understanding resulted in a passive approach which involved soaking in information rather than actively attempting to understand what was meant. Equally, when the students deployed theory with hindsight they actively attempted to understand the information offered by the people with whom they worked only once they were removed from the pressures of their face to face interactions. One student's description of her part in her interactions as that of 'a sponge' captures the passivity of these approaches to listening.

In contrast both with this sponge like approach, and with the deployment of theory as recipes for practice, in the context of the fluent approach the students were able to achieve a balance between passively soaking in and too swiftly interpreting information which involved an active attempt to make sense of information as it emerged in the course of their face to face interactions. They associated the development of this ability with a range of cognitive skills which were a further hallmark of the fluent approach, and which revolved around their approach to the use of ready made theory. Although an increasing fluency in interweaving these cognitive skills was one of the most striking features of their approach, some different strands can be separated out and examined in more detail.

In the context of the fluent approach the part played by ready made theory in the process of making sense of a situation was quite different from either of the patterns associated with the fragmented approach. In contrast with the pattern described in the previous chapter as involving the hindsight deployment of theory, the information which emerged in the course of the students' interactions with the people with whom they worked was not examined in the light of theory only after the event. Instead the students used the ready made theories on which they drew as frameworks to simultaneously guide the gathering and interpretation of information. On the other hand, ready made theories were not regarded as capable in themselves of offering complete explanations for a situation. Rather, the students emphasised the importance of assessing the likely validity of their theoretical ideas in the light of the information emerging about a particular situation. If necessary they were then able to shape and adapt their original ideas in order to take into account the particular circumstances of the people with whom they worked. It was in this sense that their approach to listening was an active rather than a passive approach. In the process of developing and adapting their original ideas in the light of emerging information the students drew as seemed appropriate on the different ideas offered by different ready made theoretical explanations. Rather than regarding different theoretical explanations as discrete, mutually exclusive bodies of knowledge, they viewed them as building blocks from which an understanding might be constructed. As one student explained it:

The systems theory gave me the bones, if you like, but the psychodynamic theory put the flesh on the bones. (Final placement student)

In addition to ideas derived from different ready made theoretical explanations, the students wove into the fabric of their custom made theories some more everyday sources of understanding. In particular, as in the context of other approaches to practice, they regarded an ability to put themselves in the shoes of the people with whom they worked as an important source of understanding. It was seen in the preceding chapter that in the context of the fragmented approach theoretical explanations and this more everyday source of understanding were treated for the most part as mutually exclusive, incompatible bodies of knowledge. Although some students did speak of resonances between the two, those resonances were treated as a source of legitimation for an unstructured, atheoretical approach. As a result their affective responses displaced their theoretical knowledge, while themselves remaining, as in the context of an everyday social approach, at the level of unchecked assumptions. In contrast, in the context of the fluent approach the students did not take it for granted that their affective responses were an accurate reflection of the feelings and needs of the people with whom they worked. Instead they were concerned to separate out their own feelings and to assess their likely validity as a source of information about the feelings and needs of the people concerned. In doing so they again made use of ready made theories to examine the origin and meaning of their feelings. This student explained something of what was involved:

> You've got to be able to put yourself in your client's shoes, otherwise it's too cold and clinical and I think you miss a lot, but at the same time once the emotions get involved things can get very cloudy. That's where the theory helps. It helps you to stand back a bit and look at your feelings in a more detached sort of way so you can see why you might be feeling certain things. Once you've got that straight you can bring the feelings back in and see what the whole makes. (First placement student)

The process described by this student was not dissimilar to the process described by Nelson-Jones in his examination of the skills required by counsellors as 'inner listening', although he makes no mention of the part which might be played in the process by the counsellor's theoretical knowledge:

> Listening, however, does not just take place between people, it also takes place *within* each person. Indeed your *inner* listening, or being appropriately sensitive to your own thoughts and feelings may be vital to your *outer* listening involving understanding another. (p.14)

The interweaving of theory and more everyday sources of understanding described above was extended in turn to an approach to experiential learning which also distinguished the fluent approach from others. In the context of other approaches few students drew on previous experiences of practice as a source of knowledge for the new situations they encountered, and those students who did so deployed ways of thinking about situations which were familiar from their previous experience on the assumption that they were applicable in every situation. In contrast, the development of the fluent approach was associated with an increasing ability to make considered use of previous experience which has some similarity with the ability to transfer learning described by Harris (1983) and Gardiner (1984), amongst others. Although the ability to transfer learning is an ability required of qualifying students, and is generally

81

recognised as an essential ability in a field of practice as wide ranging as social work, descriptions of the process involved have hitherto rested more on educational theory than on practitioners' accounts of their cognitive processes. Gardiner offers one such description:

> By the 'transfer of learning' I mean .... having an experience, recognising what is salient, the building up of patterns, making patterns of patterns which become generalisations, and then the recognition in new situations that the earlier generalisations may be appropriate or relevant. Thus, both generalisations derived from particular experiences *and* the application of these generalisations are essential components of the transfer of learning. (p.56)

While the accounts of social work practice which are the focus of this chapter have some consonance with this description, they also highlight some apparently undocumented aspects of the development of the ability to transfer learning. In particular, they suggest that in the initial stages of developing the ability ready made theory can play an important part in the formulation of generalisations. This student's description of the way in which she had made use of her previous experience provides an illustration:

> I think it starts off when you're there with your client and something rings a bell. You start to think about the content of what's being said and you tie that in with the non-verbal things. Then you think: now why is that ringing bells? You work back from there into situations you've seen before. Then you think, now what theory do I know that might connect those things? You have to bring the theory in to get a wider picture, because your analysis is only going to be as good as the experience you've got. So I would say I tend to tie it into experience first and then tie it into theory to get a wider look at it. Then you bring it back to the context to see if it gels, to see if it needs personalising. If it doesn't gel then you try to find out more. So it starts of quite intuitive, you pick it up on that level first, and that's where your experience comes in. Then it gets more analytical as you bring the theory in, but you have to personalise it again. It can't just stay as theory because it might not always fit. (First placement student)

A year later, towards the end of her education and training, the same student gave a slightly different account of the process by means of which she had made sense of the situation she described on this occasion. Although this account was unique amongst those obtained in the course of the research it was of particular interest, because it suggests that ready made theory may play a diminishing part in the transfer of learning as experience accrues:

> I think I'm drawing a lot more on my experience now. Before I was very conscious of tying my experience into theory, whereas now I can

just use the experience, because I've got the theory in there. I think what it is, is I've tied a lot of the theory to examples so I can use the example rather than going back to the theory every time. I can recognise myself doing it, it's interesting to analyse. The whole process has sort of speeded up. You've got to be careful, because no two situations are exactly alike, but at the same time the sort of things you come up against as a social worker do have a lot in common.

This description of the use of examples already linked with theory in short circuiting the process of making sense of a situation has some consonance with the findings of the study of nursing practice undertaken by Benner (1984) which were outlined in Chapter Two. As was seen there, Benner found that experienced nurses rely increasingly on what she terms paradigm cases to guide their work rather than on preconceived rules and ideas. While it is clearly not possible to draw any firm conclusions on the basis of one account, it may be that the development of expertise in social work involves a similar process within which the ability to transfer learning plays an important part.

In the course of the discussion so far it has been seen that the students were able to develop ideas about the situations they described by making use of different sources of understanding to compliment and augment each other. These ideas, however, did not in themselves constitute custom made theories. Rather the construction of custom made theory depended on a further range of skills without which the students' ideas would have been little different from the kind of speculative ideas associated with the hindsight deployment of theory. The crucial difference between that approach and the fluent approach lay in an ability on the part of the students concerned to communicate their ideas to the people with whom they worked. As was seen in the previous chapter, in the context of the fragmented approach the students had rarely attempted to explain their ideas to the people concerned. In contrast, in the context of this approach they were concerned to ensure that the people with whom they worked were aware of the direction their own thoughts were taking and were able to discuss and contribute to their ideas. The process involved had two facets. On the one hand the students made use of some of the techniques such as summarising and rephrasing information which are described in the literature of both social work and counselling to check out with the people concerned that they had understood the information offered. On the other hand they were also able to communicate ideas based on theoretical explanations to the people with whom they worked. They went about this partly by translating the specialised language associated with ready made theories into more everyday language which the people concerned could understand, and partly by offering concrete examples drawn either from their interactions with the people concerned, or from experiences with which they could associate. This student, for example, explained why she had used her client's own life experiences in order to illustrate her ideas:

83

That's one thing I've learnt, is that you can't just put your ideas onto your client and expect them to understand it in the same way you do. You've got to try and look at it through their eyes and see how you can make it make sense for them. You've got to tie it into their experiences, things they can understand. (Final placement student)

In common with their increasing ability to listen actively to the people with whom they worked, the students whose accounts are the focus of this chapter regarded their ability to communicate their ideas as a significant stage in the development of their practice. As this student put it:

When I left that meeting I was wiped out. I felt like I'd been working really hard for an hour, but I was elated too. It was the first time I'd been able to do something in an interview, to use the information that was there and put it back to them so they could see how I saw it. (First placement student)

While some considerable attention has been paid in the literature of social work practice to the reframing or rephrasing of clients' ideas, less attention appears to have been paid to how social workers might communicate theoretical ideas. In the course of the following discussion it will be seen, however, that the interweaving of both skills was the corner stone of the fluent approach.

Obtaining and interpreting information

In order to examine the ways in which the students made use of the skills described above in obtaining and interpreting information, the initial stages of their work are again considered first. It will be seen that from the outset of their work their approach enabled them to resolve the conflicts and dilemmas associated with the fragmented approach. Having examined the students' initial approach the kind of pattern which ensued is described. Finally the students' responses to questions about their eventual understanding of the situations they described are examined.

The initial stages of the students' work

As was seen in the previous chapter, in the context of the fragmented approach the students had drawn on ready made theoretical explanations in examining the information initially available to them and in developing ideas about lines of enquiry which it might be useful to pursue. In the context of the fluent approach the students' initial approach was very similar, as was the basis of their choice of theoretical explanation at this stage. Here too, where work with children and their families was concerned systems theory was usually the theory of choice, while psychodynamic theories of human development and behaviour were drawn on where work with individuals was concerned. Even at this early stage, however, the students did not expect the theories on which they drew to provide a complete explanation for the situations they were to encounter. Instead, as has been seen, they regarded their initial choice of explanation as a flexible framework to guide their exploration of the situation to hand. This conceptualisation of the role of ready made theory laid the foundation for the resolution of the conflicts and dilemmas associated with the fragmented approach.

In the first place, the students' conceptualisation of the role of theory as one of guiding rather than dictating their approach appears to have gone some way towards enabling them to resolve the conflicts between the use of ready made theory and the principles of practice espoused by social workers which were associated with the fragmented approach. That this was the case emerged not so much from what the students said about the principles of practice to which they aspired as from their accounts of the ways in which they approached their work. In the context of this approach it was in fact unusual for the students to refer explicitly to the principles of practice which underpined their approach. That they rarely did so seems to have been because they had found ways of resolving the conflicts described in the previous chapter, with the result that those conflicts were no longer a source of acute concern. The students made no mention, for example, of the sort of concerns about being judgemental or overly directive which were associated with the fragmented approach. Instead they regarded their initial ideas as sufficiently flexible to take into account their informants' own ideas and particular circumstances. As this student put it:

I know some of the jargon in family work is pretty awful, but I actually think some of it isn't as bad as it sounds. Like I never thought I'd hear myself using words like hypothesis - it sounds like you're conducting an experiment on your clients - but I've actually found it a really useful way of thinking about what you're doing. It gives you something to work from, rather than thinking where on earth do you start. It's the idea that you're just testing out ideas at this stage, not saying I'm the expert, I know what's wrong. (Final placement student)

In turn, by approaching their first meetings with a framework for guiding the gathering and interpretation of information in mind the students found that they were able to overcome the sort of concerns about the presentation of self which were associated with the fragmented approach. Because they were able to focus on identifying areas which might be explored and on planning their approach without fear of being judgemental or overly directive, they found that they were able to manage their anxiety about how they would be perceived by the people with whom they were to work. This student's response to a series of questions about how he had felt about undertaking the work he described provides an illustration:

If I'm honest my first response to the idea of taking it on wasn't all that positive. I was anxious really, I think everyone is. The first time you go out to meet a group of strangers is very daunting. I was thinking more about myself really than about the work, you know, what would they think of me, would they think I was just a useless student. ... What helped with that was the reading I'd been doing before the placement started. One of the things that came over very strongly from the community work literature was this idea of standing back from things and having a good long look around before you rush into doing anything. So I thought right, I'll get some group work books out and see what kind of things might help with that, and that's where the yardstick came from. I got some books from the library and photocopied some of the tables of the different ways groups function so I could put them together and use them as a yardstick to gauge how this group was functioning. ... I think it gave me a lot more confidence at the beginning. Before I think I wouldn't have planned it so much. I think I would have wanted to see how things went before I attempted anything more, but when you do that I think you're more anxious. I was still anxious, but I could hang onto that because the yardstick gave me something to focus on. (First placement student)

Equally, as this extract from a second account suggests, the students' recognition of the potential relevance of previous experiences of practice increased their confidence in the initial stages of their work, thus enabling them to manage some of the anxieties associated with the fragmented approach:

It made a big difference, realising that the work I'd been doing before was relevant. It gave me more confidence and I think when you're more confident you don't need to feel so much in control. (First placement student)

The flexibility of the students' initial thinking and planning greatly assisted them in resolving the conflict of aims associated with the fragmented approach. Rather than approaching their first meetings with the aim either of developing a warm relationship, or of establishing a purposeful, business like climate, they were able to approach their meetings with a clear but flexible agenda within which they could take into account the norms and conventions of social interactions without losing sight of the purpose of their work. As this extract illustrates, from their perspective, the more structured approach required to make use of theory in practice was not incompatible with the establishment of a helpful relationship:

I think your ideas are always very tentative at that stage. You have to be prepared to rethink things as you go along, but even so I think having some sort of framework to start with helps. Even in the introductory bit, you know about the weather and how I found her flat and how difficult it is to find addresses in that scheme, it helped with that because

I didn't feel I had to rush into the formal bit. ... A lot of it's confidence I think. I had an idea of the kind of things I wanted to know so it was a question of getting the balance right. Not rushing into it but not getting so carried away in the conversation that you can't get round to what you need to do. (First placement student)

Moreover, as a second extract from the same account illustrates, the use of ready made theory as a flexible framework to guide the interpretation of information enabled the students to treat the social aspects of their interactions as a potentially useful source of information, thus further closing the gap between their ideas about the establishment of a helpful relationship and the use of theory in practice:

Even while we were having coffee and chatting having an idea of the kind of things which might be important helped me to begin to sort the wheat from the chaff. You could begin to pick things out and pin them onto headings. Things about the isolation and where that fitted in with relationships and with her family. I'm not saying you should interpret everything, I mean people need to be able to talk about the weather without it having terribly deep significance, but I think there are things that come out of that kind of chit chat which can give you some indication of whether or not you're on the right lines.

The students' accounts suggest, then, that their approach to the use of ready made theory and other sources of knowledge was influential in enabling them to resolve the problems described in the preceding chapter. Further evidence to support this view emerged from their responses to questions about how their first meetings had worked out. As in the context of the fragmented approach the students had been concerned from the outset of their work to be clear with the people with whom they worked about their role and purpose. They did not achieve that aim, however, by means of a brief statement of fact, to be quickly set aside in the interests of developing a warm relationship. Nor did they expect the people concerned to be able to engage straight away in working to their own pre-determined agenda. Instead they saw the main purpose of their first meetings as one of negotiating their role and defining areas on which they might focus. In this process of negotiation their ability both to listen and to explain their own ideas played a central part. Depending on their remit and on the initial response of the people with whom they worked, the students were prepared either to take the lead by outlining their own ideas about the areas which might be explored, or to listen first to their informant's concerns. When they found it necessary to take the lead themselves their emphasis was on making sure that the people concerned had understood them and were able to express their own point of view. In the light of the information which emerged they were then able to negotiate their role. This student's description of her approach provides an illustration:

I thought if she was as withdrawn as the intake worker said she'd seemed to be I was going to have to take the lead. At the same time I didn't want to just assume that my ideas about what she needed were right. I wanted to make sure she had the chance to say what she wanted. Once she'd made coffee and we'd both relaxed a bit I started off by saying that from what the intake worker had told me there seemed to be several things worrying her. There were the bills and financial problems, but also she'd mentioned some worries about the wee boy and her relationship with his dad. I said that as far as I was concerned we could look at all those things, because it was part of my job to help with both financial and relationship problems, so perhaps we could look at what was worrying her most and decide where to start. It became pretty clear quite quickly that there was no way we were going to be able look at anything else until she felt more in control of the financial side. I think that's quite a difference actually in the way I approached it. I think before, because I had a lot of experience of working with children, I would have focussed on that instead of letting her decide. At the same time I didn't want to lose sight of the other things, because as I say I was working on this idea that we needed to look at how things had got so out of control, and I thought that might be connected with the relationship issues. I said she seemed to be most worried about the bills so I thought it would be a good idea to work on that first, but we could look at the other things later if she wanted to. (First placement student)

Equally, when their informants took the lead the students were able to listen without interrupting, begin to interpret the information offered in the light of their theoretical framework, and then negotiate their role. This student's account provides a useful illustration because he described how, taken together, his approach to the use of ready made theory and his interpersonal skills had contributed to his approach:

For the first half hour I couldn't get a word in. I think in the past I'd have been in a bit of a panic by that stage. I would probably have tried to stop them, either that or I'd have got totally lost. That's where having some sort of framework to look at it through really helped. I wasn't sitting there thinking oh my God how am I going to stop this, what am I going to say, I was actually really interested in what they were saying and how they were responding to each other. I could begin to test out some of my ideas, actually, as they were talking. When they seemed to be slowing down a bit I said something about how they'd given me a lot of information and I wanted to be sure I'd got it right, and then I told them how I'd understood what they'd been telling me. ... I didn't say right, let's look at this from a systemic perspective. It was more just a summary but reframing it a bit and then checking to make sure I'd got it right. Then I said I thought they'd done the right thing by asking for help because someone who wasn't so involved in it all could maybe help them to find a different way of dealing with it. I said that that was how I saw my part in it, rather than only working with Christopher himself, because after all I could only see him for an hour a week and they were his parents. From the way they reacted to that it was pretty clear that wasn't what they'd been expecting so I asked them what kind of help they'd been hoping for. There was quite a long silence, then his father said they'd hoped someone in authority would be able to instil a bit of sense in him. That's what I'd thought really, so I was glad he'd come out with it. I said that he was right that social workers do have powers they can use, but that that was a last resort and there were maybe some things they could try themselves. I said perhaps we could spend the next meeting looking in more detail at the things they had tried and how they'd worked out, so we could see if there was anything else they might try. They seemed reasonably happy with that. I think they were dubious about whether it would work, but I was pretty confident they'd come back and give it a try. (Final placement student)

As this account suggests, the students' use of ready made theory to guide the gathering and interpreting of information was of considerable assistance to them in working with groups of people. In contrast with the fragmented approach, in the context of this approach the students neither felt overwhelmed by the complexity of group interactions, nor resorted to hard and fast agendas in order to gain control over them. Instead they were able to use their theoretical frameworks to make sense both of the process of their interactions and of the information emerging from them. In the course of their accounts they referred to the part played by their theoretical frameworks in this process as one of enabling them to 'stand back' a little from their interactions in order to gain a wider perspective. This extract from a second account provides a further illustration:

The yardstick was incredibly useful actually because it made me more aware of - I had to think about what am I going to look for before I got there, because if I was going to be *in* the meeting I wouldn't be able to just sit back and observe. I needed to be able to play my part in the meeting and at the same time I needed to be able to stand back a bit and watch what was happening. (First placement student)

In turn, the students' approach to negotiating their role was also of assistance to them in working with groups. As was seen in the preceding chapter, in the context of the fragmented approach the difficulties experienced by the students in working with groups were compounded when conflicts of opinion occurred between the people concerned. In the context of this approach those students who encountered conflicts of opinion amongst the people with whom they worked had anticipated the likelihood of such conflict in the light of the theoretical frameworks which guided their initial approach. As a result they had been able to incorporate discussion of their own position in the process of negotiating their role. The position they negotiated for themselves was described by some students as a 'neutral' role and by others as that of a facilitator or mediator. This extract provides an illustration of what was meant:

> Another thing I wanted to achieve in that first meeting was to clarify what sort of role I would have in the family meetings, and there again the systems theory was helpful because it kept me focussed on the issues behind her coming into care. I was very aware that the problems behind that hadn't been addressed and I was pretty sure that once we started working towards her going home the same problems would start up again. If I was right, looking at how they could come to some sort of solution to that was going to be the bulk of the work, so I wanted to make it clear that I was going to be taking a neutral role, that it wasn't part of my role to decide who was right and who was wrong, but that I would be someone on the outside who could help them to listen to each other and work things out for themselves. (Final placement student)

Similarly, the students' ability to negotiate their role with the people with whom they worked appears to have been of assistance to them in overcoming some of the problems associated with statutory work. The evidence available to support this view is rather limited, because only one of the nine accounts which depicted a fluent approach was an account of work which originated in a statutory requirement for social work involvement and not in the request of the people concerned. The information contained in this account can, however, be supplemented by drawing on the accounts of other students who were able to develop some of the skills associated with the fluent approach in the course of the work they described. Taken together these accounts suggest that just as the students did not regard ready made theories as right or wrong per se, so they did not conceptualise the right to self determination as an absolute right. Again, this emerged more from their accounts of the ways in which they approached their work than from anything they said about the right to self determination. This extract from the account of statutory work which was most typical of the fluent approach suggests, for example, that by including in his negotiation of his role a clear explanation of what his statutory remit might involve the student concerned had been able to define where the boundary between his duties and his client's rights lay:

> I wanted to be clear from the start about what my statutory role meant. The way I put it was that as the work went on it might be necessary for me to wear different hats. I thought that was probably something she would understand because it's quite a common place expression. I said that whereas it was important that she felt she could use our time to talk about the things she wanted to talk about, it was also important for me to be able to bring up things I needed to bring up as part of my supervisory role. The example I gave her was the obvious one of her behaviour in the unit, that if there were problems we would need to discuss them, and that would need to come first. (Final placement student)

An extract from a second account which in other respects was less typical of the fluent approach provides a further illustration of the advantages of this approach. In this case the student concerned had initially approached her work in a way which was fairly typical of the hindsight deployment of theory. Here she described how, during her second meeting with her client's mother, she had been able to negotiate a more structured role against the background provided by a clear explanation of her statutory remit:

When I went back the next time I was able to be a lot clearer about what I was doing. I explained that because I was involved on account of people's concerns about her daughter not going to school I needed to be able to focus on that. I said I understood that a lot of other things were worrying her, and that we could look at those things too, but that perhaps we could separate the two things out a bit. I said what I'd like to do today was to concentrate on her daughter because I had the report to write, but that next week we could come back to some of the things she'd been worried about and look at how they might fit in. I think that made things clearer for her, and it definitely made it a lot easier for me, because once I'd put it that way I felt ok about bringing her back to the subject. I could reassure her that I wasn't dismissing what she was saying and we could come back to it next week. (First placement student)

Halfway through her placement another student had also been able to overcome the problems she had experienced as a result of deploying theory as recipes for practice by re-negotiating her role in order to achieve a more helpful balance between her duties and her client's rights:

The meeting before that I'd gone along with my agenda as usual, but by then I knew things were going very wrong. I should never have done what I did. He'd already identified what was making him offend, and even why he was doing it, but all I did was keep telling him what *I* thought. I still thought at that time that I had to know best, that this is what a social worker is supposed to do. ... It was a very hard way to learn, but it was good learning for me. I realised I had to get back to the basic principles of why am I here, I'm here to help you, and also to put some responsibility on him to decide what he wanted to discuss. ... It went really well. We talked about his grandparents, and, you know, I had assumed that everything was brilliant there, but it wasn't. Then he started telling me about his step-dad, and we sort of uncovered a lot of emotion about the feelings he had, which were very intense feelings. (First placement student)

These accounts suggest, then, that rather than either disowning their statutory role or setting aside their concern to respect the right of the people with whom they worked to self determination, the skills associated with the fluent approach enabled the students to achieve a balance between fulfilling their statutory duties and the rights of the people concerned. As was the case with other approaches to practice, the students' initial approach to their work was both a prelude to and a pattern for the remainder of their work. The main themes which emerged from their responses to questions about how their work had proceeded are examined next in order to illustrate the kind of pattern which ensued.

The pattern which ensued

The students' responses to questions about how their work had proceeded reveal the advantages of their initial approach. In particular, because they and the people concerned had agreed on the work to be undertaken, the students felt able to undertake that work without the intrusion of doubts about the legitimacy of their activities. At the same time, however, they placed continuing emphasis on making sure that their informants understood why they were focussing on a particular area or pursuing particular lines of enquiry. This student's description of her approach to an adoption assessment provides an illustration:

> Even though we'd spent the first meeting discussing the areas I would need to cover and they'd agreed to that, I found I had to be very careful about explaining why I needed to ask about some things when we actually came to them. I think there was a danger that because it seemed self-explanatory to me I might rush on with it without stopping to think whether they really understood why I was asking, and if I did that they might feel less able to say what they thought. The section on their personal histories was an example of that. I mentioned at the end of one meeting that we'd be moving onto that, and they said yes, they knew, but there was something about the way they said it that made me ask how they felt about that. I was glad I did because they were actually quite worried about it. Neither of them had had a particularly happy childhood and they were worried that would go against them. I think in the end I managed to put it in a way they could understand which didn't leave them feeling threatened. I tried to use specific examples they could connect with. ... One example was how the way they'd felt about school might influence things if they had a child who hated school, so it was important to look at these things ahead of time. I think that rang a lot bells, especially with him, because straight away he said, oh when you put it that way I can see why you have to look at those things. That was very much the pattern of it, making sure all the time that they understood what we were doing and why. (Final placement student)

This emphasis on continually explaining and re-negotiating the work to be undertaken also distinguished the students' approach to the discussion of difficult or painful issues. In contrast with an approach involving the hindsight deployment of theory, in the context of this approach the students were not afraid to initiate discussion of potentially difficult issues. Rather than relying on the people with whom they worked for permission to

92

address these subjects, they saw it as part of their role to create opportunities for their discussion. As this student put it:

In the past I would have been very dubious about talking about something like bereavement. I think I would have waited for them to bring it up, and even then I'm not sure I could have handled it. Now I think if you're the worker you have to take some responsibility. You can't force people to talk about things if they don't want to, but you can make sure they know the opportunity is there and you can make it as comfortable as it can be for them to do it. (Final placement student)

On the other hand, the students did not assume that difficult issues could be addressed without careful preparation. This student explained how her initial approach to negotiating her role had enabled her to prepare the ground for discussion of some issues she thought relevant:

By the third meeting the financial problems were a lot more under control, so it was a case of seeing whether she wanted to look at the relationship issues. I thought the best way to do that was by reviewing what had been achieved so far. I wanted to give her some positive feedback, because as I say I was working on the idea that the reason things had got so out of control was to do with her low self esteem. It was as if she felt powerless to take control of anything in her life. At the same time I thought that would give me the opportunity to go back to what we'd said at our first meeting about maybe looking at the relationship issues later. (First placement student)

As a second extract from the same account illustrates, in discussing difficult issues the students continued to place emphasis on explaining why they were asking particular questions, while at the same time allowing the people concerned to determine the pace of their work:

It felt like a transitional phase, like you can push it a little bit but then she's going to need her space. It seemed really important to push it a little bit by following up the lead in, but not saying I want to talk about this so that's what we're going to do, letting her go as far as she wanted to, because she was still a bit wary. There was a couple of times she'd look at me suspiciously and I said, well I'm asking about this because ... It was still a case of going very slowly, letting her know why I was asking certain things, letting her stop when she wanted to stop.

An extract from another account illustrates how a similar range of skills had assisted the student concerned in addressing issues relating to parenting and child care which had posed particular problems in the context of the fragmented approach:

I think what I've started doing is bringing in what you could call the counselling skills. I think sometimes if people listen to me they might think I'm overly theoretical. The family's so sensitive and so emotional and there's so many issues involved that sometimes I go away and draw the system out - what's happening here, why do they do that, what effect is that having over here. The difference though is going back and saying I feel this may be happening. Feeding back to people, clarifying, keeping with something even though it's painful, but letting them take their time, making sure they've understood, bringing it back all the time to why are we doing this, what are the goals, how is this relationship going to be able to function. So through that we've been able to look at the double bind messages, how it's impossible for the child to do two things at once. (Final placement student)

While enabling his client and her family to explore issues which seemed relevant in their own time, the same student had not hesitated to take a more directive approach when his statutory role seemed to require it. In response to further questioning about the skills on which he had drawn he explained how his initial approach had enabled him to combine these two facets of his role:

Apart from the counselling skills which we've talked about there was a lot to do with the exercise of personal authority. Being able to be supportive and yet also saying I have to go to the Reporter with this, or we have to look at this behaviour now. ... I don't think the behaviour was something we could not have talked about, but because we'd discussed that the first time I met her it didn't feel like a huge shift. It gave me a springboard for being able to address that with her.

It will probably be apparent that, at least from the students' own perspective, their use of ready made theory in interpreting information did not result in conflicts of opinion with the people with whom they worked. From their perspective, their approach had resulted in the development of shared ideas within which their theoretical knowledge and the views of the people with whom they worked extended and enhanced each other. This student's description of her approach provides an illustration:

I think it's really important to level with people. It's no use my having all these ideas if I don't share them with her, because that's not going to do her any good. The thing is it's no use telling your client that you think they might have low self esteem because of this theory you've been reading about. She wasn't going to understand that. What I did was I tried to tie it into the way she was when we met and the things she said. ... I think I said something like 'I've been feeling for a while now that you don't have a very good opinion of yourself'. She looked a bit taken aback at that, so then I gave her some examples of how she always seemed to give other people what they wanted, whether that was what she wanted or not. She said it was right enough, everything was done the way her boyfriend wanted and she sometimes did get pissed off with it but she still let him have his way. So then I explained that I didn't know why it was but that sometimes things that have happened when you're younger can give you a low opinion of yourself, did that ring any bells for her? That was when she started talking about her brother's death and the way that had been dealt with in the family, and it went on from there. It was really a case of giving her some ideas she could work with. Once she had the ideas she could take them and run. She left me standing sometimes, the way she was able to make connections between things. She'd bring in things I'd never even thought of. (First placement student)

Equally, the students' approach enabled them to resolve the difficulties associated with conflicts of opinion amongst the people with whom they worked which had played an influential part in shaping the fragmented approach. As was seen in the previous chapter, when the students deployed theory only with hindsight they had been able to make sense of conflicts of opinion amongst the people with whom they worked after the event, but had been unable to make use of their ideas in the course of their face to face interactions. On the other hand, when they deployed theory as recipes for practice they had felt unable to continue working together with people whose views conflicted. In contrast with either of these approaches, in the context of this approach the students' negotiation of a neutral, mediating role allowed them to make use of that role in enabling the people concerned to communicate with each other. This student's description of his approach suggests that his increasing ability to examine his own feelings had contributed to his ability to maintain the neutral stance required:

There were times when I'd find myself getting angry in meetings. The way she was treating the other members of the group was so demeaning. But I'd say to myself: watch it, remember you're supposed to be neutral here, just make sure other people get their say and don't be tempted to jump in. There again, I wasn't afraid to stop her if she was cutting other people off because I wasn't attacking her either. I was just making sure everyone there had a say, which is what I'd said I'd do. (First placement student)

In turn, by adopting and maintaining a neutral role the students were able to treat conflicts of opinion amongst the people with whom they worked as a potentially valuable source of information about the situations within which they were working. For example:

I felt very uncomfortable at first. I suppose that's a natural reaction, I mean nobody feels particularly comfortable in that kind of situation, but it was interesting too. I could feel myself constantly wanting to move out of that kind of role and having to stop myself. I think in the past I would probably have identified with the mother and supported her, but because we'd agreed this role with them I felt I could sit back a bit and look more at how the family were interacting, and that was very revealing. (Final placement student)

Overall, the students' accounts of their meetings with the people with whom they worked convey an impression of painstaking, persistent efforts to carry through the work they had negotiated to undertake. By actively striving to understand and be understood in turn, and by working to overcome barriers, whether they stemmed from their own feelings or were intrinsic to the situations they described, the students appear to have been able to achieve a balance between the establishment of a warm relationship and the pursuit of their negotiated goals. This approach was reflected in their responses to questions about their eventual understanding of the situations they described.

The students' understanding of the situations they described

As was seen at the beginning of this chapter, the students' distinctive approach to obtaining and interpreting information led to the construction of custom made theories to explain the situations they described. By drawing on different ready made theories, on previous experiences of practice and on an analysis of their affective responses, they were able to develop ideas about the situations they described which, as they emerged, were checked against the information available and explored with the people concerned. In the light of new information emerging, and particularly in the light of the responses of the people with whom they worked, the students were able to develop and extend their ideas about the situations they described. Although the different strands involved in this process have been drawn out and examined separately here, from the students' perspective they formed part of a fluid process which some students were able to describe in response to questions about how they had made sense of the situations they described. This student, for example, used both words and gestures to describe the process involved:

> I think patterns emerge, fragments of information and ideas that come together to make a pattern, so you're building a picture as you go along - no, it's less solid than a picture. It's more like two pictures one on top of the other. There's the picture in my mind, how I see it, which is made up of, just everything you know - what people say, how they are, how you feel when you're with them, how that fits with the theories you know, or other experiences you've had. Then there's the situation as they see it. It's an adjusting picture (the student began to demonstrate by sliding her hands over each other). You're holding your picture against theirs and adjusting your picture, and at the same time you're trying to show them your picture, so it's like two pictures adjusting each other. (First placement student)

On the basis of this and earlier descriptions of the fluent approach it might be thought that the development of the students' ideas had taken place only in the course of their interactions with the people concerned. This was not, however, the case. Although an increasing ability to develop and communicate ideas in the course of their interactions was a hallmark of their approach, they also spoke of the importance of written work, including both required work such as case notes or summaries and written work undertaken on their own initiative, in enabling them to formulate and develop ideas. This student's response to a question about what had helped her in making sense of the situation she described provides an illustration:

One thing was the case notes. It's only since I've been on placement that I've realised how useful case notes can be, not just to other people who might need to know what you've been doing, but actually to yourself. ... It's to do with having to make things clear for other people. It's no use rambling on, putting down every little thing, that's not going to mean much to someone else. You need to pick out the main things and see where they fit together so you can put them under headings where they belong. ... It helps you to get a better understanding yourself, because it's when you sit down and think now how does this all fit together that you can really get a good look at it and make sure there's no loose ends or things that don't add up. (First placement student)

It was seen in the preceding chapters that in the context of other approaches the difficulties experienced by the students in reaching an understanding of the situations they described were reflected in their descriptions of their written work. Conversely, in the context of this approach the students' use of written work in formulating and developing ideas was associated with an ability to develop an overview of the situations they described which was unique to the fluent approach. In place of the speculative or episodic accounts which were associated with the fragmented approach, in the context of this approach the students responded to questions about their eventual understanding with relatively succinct accounts within which their ideas were clearly presented, together with evidence to support them. In keeping with the flexibility of their approach, however, their ideas were presented not as cut and dried explanations of the situations they described, but as working models within which space was reserved for uncertainty. This student, for example, was able to give a reasonably clear account of a complex situation with reference to the different sources of information and knowledge on which he had drawn, but with the caution that some uncertainty inevitably remained:

I don't think you can ever be certain you've got it exactly right. There's always new information or things you've missed so your ideas are always changing. Having said that, you have to reach some sort of understanding, otherwise you'd be useless. ... My assessment first and foremost was that this girl's behaviour was related to her parents' marriage breaking up. They had split up when she was twelve, just as she was coming into her adolescence and needing some stability to work out her own identity. Now, if you want to know where that came from I'd have to say it was a mixture of things rather than any one theory. It was partly the systems theory and partly some of the learning from the human development lectures, but also I've seen that in a few cases, that that seems to be a very vulnerable age. What confirmed that for me was the effect her behaviour was having. I mean this was the first time her parents had spoken to each other for two years, and it came about because of her. So by her behaviour she wasn't just expressing the difficulties she was having, she was bringing them together. I don't mean that was something she was particularly conscious of, but it was there in her reaction when her father said he wasn't coming to any meetings. From what the staff said it was a very extreme temper tantrum, totally out of control. I suppose you could say that was the intuitive bit, some sense of what it must take to lose control to that extent at that age, but it added up with the other things too, it wasn't just intuition. So that was the bottom line of the assessment if you like. Behind that there was the way her mother was responding to her behaviour, and behind that again there were all the reasons why her mother was responding the way she was, things to do with her own background and her feelings about her husband. All those factors were important in deciding how best I could work with them. (Final placement student)

As this extract suggests, the ways in which the students obtained and interpreted information were closely interwoven with the ways in which they attempted to help the people concerned. This aspect of their work is now examined in the final section of the chapter.

Helping people in the context of the fluent approach

In the previous chapter it was seen that in the context of the fragmented approach the students had experienced difficulty in helping the people with whom they worked, at least from their own perspective, either because they had been reluctant to expose their own ideas or because they had expected the people concerned to cooperate in the kind of interventions which seemed rule book fashion to fit. In contrast, all those students whose accounts are the focus of this chapter thought that they had been able to help the people with whom they worked. Although the opinion of the people concerned remains unknown, the students' own accounts suggest that their approach was one which had enabled the people with whom they worked to become clearer about their situation, and hence about how the problems and needs involved might be addressed. In order to present the evidence available to support this view, the six accounts of practice which were most typical of the fluent approach will be examined first. The accounts of three students who had been able to develop the skills associated with the fluent approach in the course of the work they described will then be examined.

In two of the six cases which were most typical of the fluent approach the remit of the students concerned had involved counselling and assessment rather than any more direct approach to problem solving. One student's remit had been to counsel and assess the circumstances of a young woman who had indicated that she wanted to place the baby she was expecting for adoption. In another case the student's remit had been to counsel and assess the potential of a couple who wished to adopt a child. In these cases the students had been able to draw on their ability both to make sense of information as it emerged, and to explain their own ideas in fulfilling the dual purpose of their involvement. In turn, from their perspective at any rate, not only their own assessment but also their clients' understanding was enhanced. This student's response to a question about how her work had left her feeling provides an illustration:

I'm pleased with the way it all came together. I think they did most of it themselves but there were some things I had more of a spoke in. I think getting them to think things through themselves, encouraging that analytical ability, helping them make the links, that was my part. When they started to do that for themselves, linking with the past, linking with their nephews and nieces, that felt good because it felt like I'd enabled them to do that. After that writing the report wasn't nearly as daunting as it seemed. It was like you've got the guide lines, you've got the theories, and now you've got the information to fill that out. It had gone from being a generalised assessment to being an assessment of this particular couple. (Final placement student)

In the remaining four cases the students' work had involved a more direct problem solving remit. In two cases their approach to helping the people concerned had nevertheless remained centred on enabling them to become clearer about about how the problems they faced might be addressed. This student, for example, thought that his ability to maintain a neutral stance and to make use of information as it emerged in the course of their interactions had played a part in enabling his client's parents to change the ways in which they dealt with their son's behaviour:

What pleased me most was that I'd been able to use what was there, I was able to use that as a tool rather than getting caught up in it. I was pleased when it worked, which I think it did. When they came back the following week they said straight away that things were a lot better. ... From a position where this kid honestly had nothing left to lose in terms of sanctions they could apply they'd started to build that back up. You could see it in the way they were together too. They were treating him as if they were proud of him instead of putting him down all the time. In fact his dad said it. When I said how pleased I was things were better, his dad said well it's Chris too you know, he's made a real effort. (Final placement student)

A second student had brought to bear the skills which were the hallmark of the fluent approach in working both individually and jointly with his client and her mother. In this complex piece of work his approach to the use of ready made theory and other sources of knowledge enabled him not only to develop an overview of their situation, but also to respond flexibly to their individual needs while working towards the goal they had identified:

> It was one of the most complicated pieces of work I've done. I don't think anyone in the office expected her to be able to leave care. In fact several people when they heard I'd been allocated this case said I'd been taken a loan of because there was no chance of doing any work there. What helped me there though was this idea I talked about earlier that you can use more than one theory without losing sight of what you're working towards, which was to get this family, not just back together, but able to live together too. Now, to do that the mother and daughter had to be able to see each other's point of view a lot more than they did, but there were things blocking that so my idea was to work with them both as individuals and use the family meetings to bring it all together. ... That's where the objective stance I talked about paid off. Because I was working with them both as individuals it would have been quite easy I think to get drawn in, but I was clear and they were clear that I was there to help them talk to each other. ... I'm fairly pleased with the way it worked. She's been back at home for two weeks now, which nobody thought was possible. I'm pretty sure they'll still have a lot of ups and downs. I think they'll still need quite a bit of support, but I don't think she'll be back in care again. (Final placement student)

In these cases, then, the students' approach to helping the people with whom they worked was largely synonymous with their approach to obtaining and interpreting information. In two further cases, however, the students concerned had combined the skills associated with the fluent approach with some more direct ways of helping. In contrast with the interventions associated with the deployment of theory as recipes for practice, these ways of helping were not derived directly from the ready made theories which had guided their initial approach. Rather, in keeping with the ways in which they constructed custom made theories to explain the situations they described, the students combined different sorts of intervention to devise ways of helping the people with whom they worked which were tailored to their specific situation. For example, one student had employed a task centred approach in helping her client regain control of her financial affairs as a prelude to exploring with her the reasons behind her loss of control. As her response to a question about the strengths of her approach indicates, the student did not regard these two approaches as mutually exclusive. Instead she regarded them as approaches which both made sense in terms of her developing overview of her client's situation:

> I think being able to combine the two things, the financial problems and

the relationship problems. I think in the past I wouldn't have spent much time on the financial problems. I would probably have sorted that out for her so we could get on to the things I thought were important. The way it worked out was good, because it gave me some indication of how capable she could be, and it gave her some back some control. I think that was important when it came to the other problems, because she'd already seen that she could achieve something. (First placement student)

As a second extract from her account illustrates, the student thought that her combined approach had enabled her client to find new ways of addressing her problems:

I knew I was almost finished when she told me she'd had a long talk with her boyfriend. She'd been able to tell him what she wanted from their relationship and what she expected of him as a father, that he couldn't just come and go as he pleased. I knew then I was almost finished, because she'd actually asserted herself for the first time and said what she wanted.

In another case the student concerned had also combined the skills associated with the fluent approach with some more direct ways of helping:

The thing I was most pleased about was that they'd done it for themselves. What I'd done was to make sure everyone who wanted to could have a say, and perhaps there was a bit of modelling in that because some people had begun to speak out more themselves when she was dominating the proceedings. Also I think they'd begun to see that by using procedures like agendas everyone could see, they could make sure things weren't being rushed through or skipped according to one person's whim. The idea of holding elections, though, that was their own idea. They organised it themselves, and even though she was re-elected at that stage, I knew that was a beginning. When I left the AGM I thought that's it, it's their group now, not hers. It took a few more weeks but I think it was that feeling that they could do something about it which eventually made them able to challenge her and insist that she retract what she'd written or resign. (First placement student)

In contrast with the fragmented approach, then, in the context of this approach the students were not dependent solely on the ways in which the people with whom they worked understood and responded to the situations they were in. Neither, however, did they expect them to cooperate unquestioningly in the kind of interventions which seemed rule book fashion to fit. Instead they created opportunities for the people concerned to explore their situations, and enabled them, in some cases by combining more direct ways of helping with their exploratory approach, to become clearer about and find ways of addressing the problems or needs involved. Having done so, however, they did not assume that the people concerned needed no further help. Rather, as this extract illustrates, they were concerned to explore the implications and to offer support when it seemed likely to be needed:

> I could see how pleased they were with what they'd done, and I didn't want to undermine that. All the same, I was aware that this could be a bit of a honeymoon period and that if he started behaving badly again they might need quite a bit of support to keep going. What I did was, I suggested that because things were so much better we could maybe meet once a fortnight instead of once a week to review how things were going. Then if they felt things were ok at the end of six weeks we could look at ending it. (Final placement student)

Further support for the view that the skills associated with the fluent approach played some part in enabling the students to be of assistance to the people with whom they worked emerges from three accounts which were somewhat less typical of the approach. In each of these three cases the students concerned had come up against the kind of problems which were associated with the deployment of theory as recipes for practice, but had been able to resolve those problems by bringing into play some of the skills associated with the fluent approach. In one case the student concerned had initially approached her work with a family from a systemic perspective. In common with many other students she had found that she was unable to secure the cooperation of all members of the family. Rather than abandoning her original perspective, however, she had treated the failure of her attempt at family work as a source of information in the light of which she had adapted and extended her ideas:

> One of the things I've realised is that you can use a theory without having to act it out. It was becoming increasingly obvious that this family simply couldn't work together. They literally could not sit in the same room and concentrate on anything for more than two minutes. Then he started not coming to meetings and she was coming on her own with the children. Finally it dawned on me: this family are telling us something. That's when we agreed that I'd work alone with the mother instead of it just happening. I think in the past I would have dropped the systemic approach at that stage and gone back to the more therapeutic sort of approach I was familiar with, but what I learnt was that you can do both. ... I think a lot of the learning was about the value of the therapeutic relationship, not in the sense of making wonderful interpretations, which I think is what I'd thought it was about, but just being with someone, listening quietly - holding is the word that comes to mind. But within that relationship I could use the systems theory to look at it with her. ... It's this business of empowering again. Thinking about her very depressed state, there was no sense of control over what was happening to her and the kids. It was trying to break that down a bit into what's good for you, what's good for him, what's bad for you, what's bad for him. I think that helped her to see herself in a less passive light. Certainly she's a different woman now from the

depressed, cowed person she was. She got her own tenancy a couple of weeks ago, and she's planning to move out with the kids at the weekend. I'll find out next week whether she has actually moved, but I think she will. If she doesn't it's not a disaster. We can use that to look again at what's keeping her in the relationship, what she might want to change. (Final placement student)

In another case the student concerned had been able to overcome the problems she experienced in undertaking development work by adapting her methods to take into account the perspective of the other professionals involved:

I'll tell you, I was very idealistic about it to begin with. I thought they were just going to fall at my feet. Then I started thinking why are they like this, and I think it's partly a defence you know, working with sick children they're under a lot of stress. ... I think that came from the reading but also when I worked with mentally handicapped people, I had my own defences and I was really conscious of them. The things they said too. One nurse said, about the children crying you know, she said you get as hard as nails. Also one of the nurses in ENT, she said to me they're seen as baddies, and I think that's true. They're seen as baddies by the children and by the doctors. So I started thinking, how can I show them without making them feel like baddies. The way I did it was I asked them to keep a diary in the ward to pass on information about play so I wasn't coming in at the back of them duplicating their work. Which was true, because that was happening, that some children were getting a lot of attention and others got none. That worked well. They write in it every day so they're thinking about what they're doing. I think it's the sort of thing they're used to doing anyway, it fits in with their routines and all. (Final placement student)

The third student described how he had been able to resolve the problems he had encountered in implementing a task centred approach by augmenting this method of intervention with an analysis of his negative feelings about his client's failure to cooperate:

The main thing I've learned from this work is that thing about how you can use your feelings. Every week I'd go round and find he'd done nothing he was supposed to do. He'd meet me at the door with yet another sheaf of brown envelopes and expect me to sort it out. I was getting very irritated by it. Nothing I suggested seemed to make any difference and I was beginning to think there wasn't a lot of point to going on with it. It was the theory that helped me there. I was doing some reading about transference and all that, so I was standing back and looking at it in a more general way. I could see how the way he was making me feel might be a reflection of the way he was feeling: powerless and threatened. Once I'd seen that I could see how to deal with it. That's where the idea of taking the one down position came in.

It was honest too, it wasn't just a ploy. What I did was the next time he met me with a pile of bills I told him I was stuck, I'd tried everything I could think of and I was stuck. He said you're a lot of use aren't you? But the next time I went round he'd been on the phone to the lawyer and the bank, and he was sorting it out. ... No thanks to you, was how he put it but that didn't worry me, because it meant he was left feeling he'd done it himself. And he had. (First placement student)

There is some evidence, then, in the accounts which have been the focus of this discussion that the cognitive and interpersonal skills associated with the fluent approach played some part in enabling the students to be of assistance to the people with whom they worked. The main features of the approach are summarised below.

Summary

The approach to practice described in this chapter was differentiated from the fragmented approach on the basis of the students' approach to the use of theoretical and other sources of knowledge in making sense of the situations they described. In contrast with the conflicts of knowledge which were the hallmark of the fragmented approach, in the context of this approach the students drew on ready made theories and other sources of understanding in constructing custom made theories to explain the situations they described. A range of cognitive and interpersonal skills underpinned their ability to construct this type of theory, including:

- an ability to listen and actively make sense of information as it emerged in the course of an interaction;

- an ability to develop ideas by drawing not only on different ready made theories but also on other sources of knowledge to compliment and augment each other;

- an ability to communicate and discuss ideas with the people concerned.

These cognitive and interpersonal skills enabled the students to overcome the conflicts of knowledge from which the problems associated with the fragmented approach stemmed. In turn, the construction of custom made theories to explain the particular situations they described was associated with an ability to arrive at an overall understanding of those situations which was unique to the fluent approach. Equally, from the students' perspective at least, their skills had enabled them to be of assistance to the people with whom they worked.

7 The part played by academic teaching

Both the students' accounts of their work and their responses to direct questions about their education and training suggest that although course content had been influential in enabling them to move beyond the everyday social approach, some of the teaching methods employed were less than helpful in enabling them to overcome the problems associated with the fragmented approach. The first section of this chapter examines the ways in which course content influenced the development of the students' practice, while in the second section the strengths and limitations of the teaching methods employed are considered.

Course content

The students' accounts suggest that four topics covered in the course of academic teaching had been of assistance in enabling them to move beyond the everyday social approach. Prominent amongst these were the teaching provided about human development and family work. As was seen in Chapter Five, the theoretical explanations to which the students most commonly referred in the course of their accounts were psychodynamic explanations of human development and explanations associated with a systemic perspective on family work. Although some students indicated that previous experiences of practice or practice teachers had been their main source of information about these explanations, the great majority indicated that academic teaching during the first year of their course had been either an additional or a main source of information. As the following extract illustrates, the significance attributed by the students to this teaching revolved around their perception that it had given them words for or otherwise heightened their awareness of facets of the social world which they had previously taken for granted in a way typical of the everyday social approach:

The ideas might have been there, but I wouldn't have had the labels. I wouldn't have used words like 'dynamic', it would just have been a couple. The ideas might have been there, but because I didn't have the labels they wouldn't have been as explicit so I wouldn't have thought of discussing them.

While teaching on human development and family work emerged from the students' accounts as particularly influential, the provision at the beginning of their course of teaching related to principles of practice also appears to have played a part in enabling them to move beyond the everyday social approach. The students attributed to this teaching, in conjunction with the first essay they were required to submit, a heightened awareness of the values on which they based their approach to their work. For example:

It's this self determination thing. In a way I suppose it's been hanging around for years but it suddenly comes up. I think the lectures and the first essay were very good for that. I think the way I used to work, it was 'we'll solve their problems and then give them a bit of self determination', whereas it's come to me a lot more that they've got as much right to be involved in solving them.

As was seen in Chapter Five, a heightened awareness of values, reflected in the students' references to the principles of practice to which they aspired, was one of the features which distinguished the fragmented approach from the everyday social approach. In this respect the students' perceptions of the influence of their education and training concur with the conclusion drawn by Wright (1985) on the basis of a review of research in this area, that rather than inculcating new values social work training develops an already established value base.

Finally, in addition to their heightened awareness of principles of practice, the students also attributed to teaching during the first year of their course a heightened awareness of other ways in which social work interactions might be managed, for example the ways in which questions might be phrased in exploring clients' situations. Responses such as this to questions about changes in their interviewing skills suggest that in this respect too academic teaching had been influential in enabling the students to move beyond the everyday social approach:

Student I think that's the kind of thing that's like conversation anyway. A lot of it's intuitive, picking up cues. I think the difference is it was a lot more structured than it would have been before. The course makes you a lot more conscious about what you're doing.

J.S. Can you give me an example?

Student Open questions! Keeping it open. It was a different sort of interview. I think I would have been a lot more talkative before the course. In a way it's been separating me the very talkative, me the personal and getting a bit more professional here, the social worker.

Whereas before it's been 'let's all have a conversation', this was 'we're having an interview here and it's got to have some structure.

In contrast with those aspects of course content which have been discussed above, two aspects were singled out by the students as particularly disappointing. These were the teaching provided about group work and about issues relating to race and gender. Because the students' concerns about teaching in these areas were closely bound up with their experiences of the teaching methods employed they will be examined in the course of the following discussion.

Teaching methods

Both the students' accounts and their responses to direct questions about their education and training suggest that an emphasis on traditional teaching methods imposed limitations on the extent to which they were able to make use of course content in practice. This is not to suggest that their teachers used only traditional teaching methods. On the contrary, the course outline provided for students, which was summarised in Chapter Two, demonstrates that a variety of teaching methods were employed. From the students' perspective, however, the balance was weighted in favour of more traditional methods which appear to have been of limited help to them in integrating course content with other sources of knowledge and in developing the interpersonal skills required to make use of course content in practice. The main problems encountered by the students in this respect concern the volume and organisation of the information presented, a perceived emphasis on the lecture as a vehicle for presenting information, and, as a corollary of the latter, a lack of attention to their own experience, values and attitudes. Each of these problematic areas will be considered in turn before going on to examine the students' experiences of some of the other teaching methods discussed in the course of the research interviews.

The volume and organisation of information

Within the literature of social work education growing recognition of the problems involved for both teachers and students in coping with the volume of material to be encompassed within the curriculum has led to interest in innovatory curriculum designs. Sainsbury (1982), proposes, for example, that a thematic approach within which generic problems are discussed in relation to different theoretical perspectives might help students to make better use of theory in practice. More recently, Burgess and Jackson (1990) have described the introduction at Bristol University of a version of this kind of thematic approach which seems more radical than Sainsbury's proposal, in that it aims to involve students in actively defining their learning priorities and addressing them through a range of learning resources. As was seen in Chapter Two, other suggestions revolve around a concern to stimulate the inductive development of theory grounded in students' experiences of practice.

Although it will be argued in Chapter Nine that a great deal more research is required before it can be claimed with any certainty that this kind of innovatory curriculum is more helpful for the development of students' practice, the accounts of the students who took part in this research do suggest that too great a volume of material to be learnt was unhelpful, in that the problems involved led to their abandoning the attempt. As will be clear from the preceding discussion, those aspects of course content which were helpful in relation to the development of their practice were derived from teaching during the first year of their course. Noticeably absent from the majority of the students' accounts was any reference to the many areas covered during the second year of their course. This may be partly because much of this content was concerned with different client groups, with the result that some of the areas covered would inevitably be less directly relevant than others to the work described by each student. The students' responses at the end of training to more general questions about their experience of their course suggest in addition, however, that they had been overwhelmed by the amount of information provided during the two years of their course, and particularly during the second year. For example, comments such as 'in the end you just give up trying to take it all in, you just do the minimum for the essays' were very common. Moreover, responses like this suggest that the organisation of the material presented into discrete subject areas compounded the problems the students experienced in coping with the amount to be learnt:

> I mean you get sociology thrown at you, you get psychology thrown at you, you get social policy thrown at you, you get human development thrown at you, and then you get twenty seven client groups thrown at you. Now there may be a lot of information there that's useful and valid, but there's no way of linking it together. It's all divided up separately and I find it difficult to learn from that. I needed a map, something to make it make sense.

In addition to the problems involved in making sense of the information presented on their course, it seems possible that the conceptual model implicit in the way the information was organised may have played a part in some cases in developing or perpetuating the absolutist conceptualisation of theory which was a hallmark of the fragmented approach. As was seen in Chapter Five, in the context of this approach the students conceptualised the theoretical ideas to which they referred as discrete bodies of knowledge which in themselves offered either a correct or an incorrect explanation for the situations they described. From their perspective, however, this was the way in which the ideas to which they referred had been presented to them. As one student put it:

> There's no attempt made to look at why you might choose to believe one

theory or another. It's an implausible model. None of these theories are watertight, yet they're taught as if they are.

The significance of individual comments of this kind was strengthened at a meeting held to obtain the students' views on the validity of the material presented in the preceding chapters, where a request for their reactions to what is now Chapter Five was met by a deluge of comments to the effect that 'the course teaches theory as recipes for practice'.

The lecture as a vehicle for presenting information

In common with traditional ways of organising the social work curriculum, the use of the lecture as a vehicle for presenting information has recently received attention within the literature of social work education from writers who have explored the relevance of educational principles and theories for this field. The consensus of opinion appears to be that this teaching approach is associated with passive, reproductive approaches to learning which may be incompatible with the demands of social work practice. Harris (1985) suggests, for example, that teaching methods which demand more active approaches to learning will equip students more appropriately for practice:

> The demands of active learning are such as to avoid the worst elements of the master-pupil relationship, emphasising students' responsibility for finding solutions rather than being given them - a task more closely related to the demands of practice than passive learning. (p.87)

Although it will be seen shortly that the students' course clearly recognised the value of teaching methods designed to allow them a more active role, the emphasis, from the students' own perspective, remained on presenting information through the medium of lectures. An indication of the strength of this perception is contained in the fact that sixteen of the nineteen students who were interviewed at the end of training singled out an emphasis on lecturing as amongst the most disappointing features of their course. The difficulties involved in absorbing the amount of information presented by some lecturers, and the boredom of sitting and listening for the required amount of time were frequent complaints. The main thrust of the students' comments, however, concerned an important corollary of the perceived emphasis on lecturing, namely a lack of attention to their own experience, to their values and attitudes, and to the question of how they might make use of course content in practice. It will probably already be apparent from the preceding chapters that the students' concerns about how to use course content in practice were wide spread, and that the problems involved lay at the heart of the fragmentation of knowledge depicted in many of their accounts. To elaborate the point here therefore seems unnecessary. Their other concerns do, however, require some elaboration in order to draw out the implications for the development of their practice.

The lack of attention paid to their own life and work experiences was a constantly recurring theme in the students' responses to questions about their education and training. From their perspective, academic teaching on their course had failed to help them to make sense of and build on this experience, and this, together with an emphasis on new learning, had left them feeling devalued and deskilled. The vehemence of this student's response to a question about her experience of the first year of her course was very striking, because throughout the preceding segments of the interview she had been quietly spoken and had talked at some length about her timidity and lack of confidence:

> I've learnt far more from my placement than from the school learning. I think through experiencing something I learn more, whereas the course dismisses your experience as if what went before wasn't important. 'You're now back to learn how to do it properly', that's the attitude. Whereas a lot of what we were doing was good work. It was important work, and it was hard work. Try telling them that. They pay lip service to it, but they don't listen.

The resentment expressed by this student was echoed by most of the students who took part in the research. Although it might be thought that these feelings would have subsided later in training, as the students adapted to their role as learners, this was not the case. Rather, their feelings persisted to the end of training. In the words of three final placement students, they felt they had been treated 'like kids', 'like undergraduates', and 'like empty slates, dummies with no experience of anything'. In some cases the students' resentment had played a significant part in their rejection of theoretical ideas in favour of more everyday understandings. As was seen in Chapter Five this led to a vicious circle within which an unstructured, atheoretical approach was legitimated on the grounds that there was little need to use theory in practice. More widespread, however, were the difficulties experienced by the majority of students who took part in the research in achieving an appropriate transfer of learning. Within the literature of social work education Badger (1985) and Evans (1985), amongst others, have described attempts to enable students to transfer learning gained prior to training to the new situations they encounter during training. The accounts of the students who took part in this research suggest that this kind of approach would have been both welcome and beneficial.

In contrast with their concerns about the lack of attention paid to their own life and work experiences, which emerged at an early stage of their education and training, the students' concerns about the lack of attention paid to their values and attitudes did not emerge in most cases until the end of training. As has been seen, during the first year course content and written work relating to principles of practice had heightened their awareness of the values which underpined their work, and at the end of their first placement most students expressed considerable satisfaction with this aspect of their course. By the end of training, however, the students were very much less satisfied. Their responses to questions at this stage suggest that while work in the first year on principles of practice had been greatly appreciated, its effect in the longer term had been to induce a comforting sense of the consonance of their values with those of their chosen profession which they later wished had been challenged. Although a series of seminars on social philosophy during the second year of their course had begun to provide the challenge they wanted, from the students' perspective this was too little too late. Amongst some more general concerns they were particularly concerned about the lack of attention paid to issues of gender and race. This student's feelings on the subject were widely shared:

> The most disappointing thing for me is that you're not challenged at all. It's as though we all come to the course wearing our nice social work values on our sleeves, and I expected to be challenged on that. We've had some good seminars this year on ethics. The tutor was good at playing devil's advocate and that was good, but it really only began to scratch the surface. In the other classes it's marginalised. Like the workshops on gender and race. They say it's implicit in everything on the course, but it isn't, it's marginalised.

While the students themselves expressed dissatisfaction with the lack of attention paid to their values and attitudes, the implications for their ability to negotiate the moral complexities of practice which had posed problems for many students, particularly in relation to statutory work, emerged from their responses at the end of training to questions about the sort of work for which they felt most and least prepared. Of the nineteen students who were interviewed at this stage only six said they felt reasonably prepared to undertake statutory work. Four of these students attributed their relative confidence in this area of work to their placement experiences, and particularly to the practice teaching approaches they encountered, while two further students attributed their relative confidence to pre-training experience in area teams. The remaining thirteen students expressed unease at the prospect of undertaking statutory work, and the most common explanations given revolved around their inability to reconcile this type of work with the principles of practice to which they aspired.

It was seen in Chapter Six that an ability to integrate theoretical ideas, principles of practice and other sources of knowledge was a hallmark of the fluent approach. It seems possible, then, that an emphasis on lecturing, and a concomitant lack of attention to the students' own experience as well as to their values and attitudes, may have played some part in developing or perpetuating the fragmentation of knowledge depicted in many of their accounts.

111

As was noted earlier, lectures were not the only teaching method the students encountered in the course of their education and training. From their perspective, however, the other methods used were either less than successful or insufficient to meet their learning needs. One of the commonest methods employed in an attempt to enable the students to play a more active part in their course was, from their perspective, the least successful. This involved the use of a lecture format followed by discussion of the material presented. Thirteen of the students interviewed at the end of training singled out this approach as one which had failed to help them learn, and their comments revolved around two main issues. In the first place some students felt that this approach had confused lecture with seminar and in doing so diminished what might be achieved by either. As one student put it:

> I'm not saying I like being lectured at, nobody does, but that might have been better than trying to get us to discuss things in the big group. At least you'd know where you were. To me the course confuses lectures with seminars and I don't think that works. Either you give a lecture and acknowledge that's what you're doing, or you let the students present things and bring our experience in that way. The seminars in social philosophy were more like that, and the special interest group this term was good because it was up to us to present things, but the way most people did it you were expected to latch onto whatever topic it was and that doesn't work.

The second issue raised by the students about group discussions concerned the dynamics which operated in the student group. While some students spoke of the difficulty they had in speaking in a large group, and of a sense that when they did speak their contributions were not valued by some of their fellow students, others spoke of the frustration they felt at being one of a few people who were willing to contribute when the majority of students did not. This schism between 'talkers' and 'non-talkers' was a troubling phenomenon for the students, and it was something they would have welcomed help with from their teachers. From their perspective, however, group dynamics were an area which was scarcely addressed by their teachers, or at least not in a way which might have helped them to explore their own responses to group interactions. This extract provides an illustration of their concerns:

> I think what happened was we all got into roles very early in the course and we couldn't get out of them. We tried to address that ourselves, as a group, because the course doesn't look at that, but it felt very awkward. Even though it was just students there the only people who talked were the ones who talk anyway. We needed some facilitation, someone to help us look at that. There's hardly anything on groups in the course, and what there was, it was all other people. Like this applies to clients but

not to us. There was nothing to help us look at ourselves, how we work in a group.

As has been seen, the students experienced considerable difficulties in working with groups, particularly family groups, which were associated with their own responses to group interactions. In these circumstances the provision of opportunities to explore their responses during their education and training might have made a helpful contribution to the development of their practice. As far as the teaching methods which were employed are concerned, it is perhaps unsurprising, given their concerns about large group discussions, that the students much preferred a second approach which was also commonly used to supplement a lecture format. This involved dividing into smaller groups to discuss the information which had been presented. Several students again felt, however, that the absence of facilitation had limited what could be achieved. When this approach was combined with role play or exercises in twos and threes it was appreciated more.

One aspect of academic teaching on the students' course which it might be thought would have gone some way towards addressing the concerns they identified was the provision throughout their education and training of tutorial teaching. Although there seems to an assumption that this form of teaching constitutes an important aspect of social work education and training little attention appears to have been paid to it in the literature of the field. Stone (1982, p. 49), for example, alludes to the tutor as 'an influential figure' in students' lives, but does not elaborate further. Contrary to this kind of assumption, however, tutorial teaching does not emerge from the accounts of the students who took part in this research as a particularly significant aspect of their education and training, since only two students mentioned their tutor as having contributed to the development of their practice. In one case a tutor had a particular interest in the type of work being undertaken by a student and had been able to offer support and suggestions for reading which had been of direct assistance. In the second case a tutor had been involved in helping to resolve problems which had arisen in the course of a placement, and this was described by the student concerned as having a direct influence on the development of his practice. For the most part, however, tutorial teaching was not mentioned by the students except in response to direct questioning. From their responses it emerged that some students had found tutorials problematic because from their perspective their tutor's approach had not enabled them to address their learning needs. While opinions about individual teaching approaches are perhaps particularly open to personal bias, there was a considerable degree of consensus amongst students who shared the same tutor about the extent to which his or her approach had been helpful. Moreover, it will be seen in the following chapter that the kind of approaches to tutorial teaching which the students found unhelpful were very similar to practice teaching approaches which they found less

113

than helpful. This suggests that some approaches to individual teaching were generally found more helpful than others.

Three approaches to tutorial teaching were perceived to be less than helpful by the students. These included an approach which had involved the establishment of a relationship which they found difficult to distinguish from a therapeutic relationship. Although they appreciated the warmth of this approach the students concerned felt that it was insufficiently challenging. A similar opinion was expressed by other students who found their tutor warm and approachable, but who felt that tutorials had remained at the level of general conversation. In contrast with these warm but unchallenging approaches the third approach which the students found less than helpful was an approach which they described as rather distant and overly intellectual. The students who encountered this approach indicated that they had felt rather intimidated by it, and had therefore been reluctant to discuss any problems they were experiencing during tutorials.

Unsurprisingly, given these perceptions of unhelpful approaches, the kind of approach which was unanimously considered helpful by those students who encountered it was one which was perceived to combine warmth and a personal interest in the students as individuals with a more challenging approach to identifying both strengths and learning needs. Even in those cases where a tutor's approach was perceived to have been helpful, however, this seems to have had little direct influence on the development of the students' practice. It was not the case, for example, that those students who perceived their tutor's approach to be helpful were predominantly those who developed a fluent approach to practice. Nor did these students refer to tutorials in the course of their accounts as a significant aspect of their education and training. The reason seems likely to lie at least in part in the fact that from the students' perspective tutorials had taken place too infrequently to have very much significance. This student's comment was not untypical:

> When I came on the course I'd expected there would be a lot more attention to you as an individual. I don't know why, I just assumed that's what a social work course would be like. I know tutorials are supposed to do that, but they don't happen very often. I actually had more tutorials when I was an undergraduate. My tutor was very good, and I got a lot out of the tutorials I had, but in the end of the day I'm not sure it made a lot of difference. There's only so much you can do in two or three at the most tutorials a term.

One corollary of the lack of time available for tutorial teaching which was mentioned by several students concerned their practice based written work. Although attention appeared to have been paid in tutorials to how they might approach this work, the attention paid to the end result was limited to written comments. While some students would have appreciated discussion of the practice issues raised in these comments, others would have welcomed assistance in developing the skills involved in analysing and structuring the material they had presented. This student, for example, was aware of some problems in this respect:

I feel that I tend to write in a very prosaic way. Everything is a story. I felt when I was trying to write the dissertation that I was in danger of producing my stream of consciousness about the work, rather than step back and look at it and say what was important for me or others was x, y, z. The thing is that to stand back from it and say what is important you've got to know what is important to your assessor so you can structure your work in a way that makes sense to them and to you.

Given the difficulties experienced in analysing and organising information not only by this student, but also by many of the other students who took part in the research, more attention to the form as well as to the content of their written work might have contributed not only to the quality of their academic work, but also to the development of their practice.

In contrast with the teaching methods so far discussed, two further methods were identified by all the students who took part in the research as having made a significant contribution to the development of their practice. The first of these was the inclusion of contributions from practitioners to supplement information presented by lecturers. This approach appears to have gone some way towards meeting a need identified by many students for role models who could demonstrate how particular theories and techniques might be used in practice. An indication of the potency of such role models is provided by the fact that practitioners' contributions were frequently mentioned by the students as having been a source of inspiration and information in undertaking the work they described. Even towards the end of their education and training, for example, some students referred back to a session during the first year of their course in which a group of practitioners had demonstrated how they speculated about the meaning of the information available when working with families. As this extract indicates, this had been a lasting source of learning:

It's a long time ago now, but whenever I'm stuck like that I think back to this session we had in the first year where these practitioners came in and showed us how they worked. ... It was the idea that you could speculate, that you didn't have to have all the answers. I use that a lot. It's better if you can do it with someone else, but even on my own I can use that to free my mind up a bit: ok, this doesn't seem to be working, let's sit down and throw some ideas around.

The only complaint the students had about this kind of input was that there was not enough of it, and this was also their only complaint about a teaching approach which was unanimously agreed to have been the most helpful. This was the use, during the second term of their course, of video taped role play in skills teaching. In the students' opinion this teaching was the only aspect of academic teaching on their course other than contributions from practitioners which had helped them to address the question which was of greatest concern to them, namely how they might make use of course content in practice. They particularly appreciated the fact that this work was undertaken in small groups, where as one student put it 'you could make a fool of yourself without feeling stupid'. They also very much appreciated the opportunity to observe and reflect on their practice with the help of criticism and suggestions from their teachers and fellow students. Again, the potency of this teaching method is illustrated by the fact that in the course of their accounts several students singled out work undertaken in a skills class as having enabled them to overcome some of the problems associated with the fragmented approach. For example:

> It was the skills class that helped me there. ... What happened was, the tutor asked if anyone had anything they wanted to work on. I thought it's now or never, so I said I was having a lot of problems with this case. So then we role played that meeting. The first time I played myself, the social worker, and then we did it again exactly the same, only this time I played the son and someone else played the social worker. It was incredible. I suddenly realised how he must have felt with me and his mother both getting on at him like that. Then people made suggestions how I could handle it differently and we tried some of those until I felt comfortable with it. That was a breakthrough for me, that class.

As far as the students were concerned, this kind of teaching met their learning needs exactly and without exception they felt that they would have benefitted greatly had it been extended throughout the two years of their course. As one student put it:

> You can learn more in one twenty minute role play than in twenty months of lectures.

Or as another student put it:

> The skills class was brilliant. It was the only part of the course that looked at you yourself, and after all that's all you've got.

Overall, then, the impression conveyed both by the students' accounts and by their experiences of academic teaching is that by emphasising the coverage of course content at the expense of attention to the teaching methods employed, their teachers may, paradoxically, have imposed limitations on the extent to which the students were able to learn how make use of course content in practice. As a corollary, the development of the students' practice beyond the fragmented approach appears to have depended largely on their placement experiences. These are discussed in the following chapter.

8 The part played by practice placements

As was noted in the introductory chapter, this research was carried out against a background of rapid change in the field of social work education, including moves towards the accreditation of practice teachers and the approval of placement agencies. The accounts of the students who took part in the research suggest that this attention to the quality of placement learning is not misplaced. In particular, the teaching approaches they encountered while on placement appear to have had a considerable influence on the development of their practice. In some cases, however, factors associated with their placement agencies also played a significant part. The influence of both aspects of the students' placement experiences is therefore discussed in the course of this chapter.

The students' experiences of practice teaching

Of the nineteen students who were interviewed towards the end of their final placement, fourteen students had encountered approaches to practice teaching during one or more of their placements which have so close a resemblance to the objectionable approaches described by Rosenblatt and Mayer (1975) that it was unnecessary to develop a new terminology to describe them. By the end of training only one of these students had developed a fluent approach to practice. The conclusion suggested, that these approaches were unhelpful in relation to the development of their practice, is supported by the fact that the other five students who had developed a fluent approach had all encountered a more helpful approach during each of their three placements. The four approaches which appear to have been less helpful are discussed here first, together with their implications for the development of the students' practice. The relationship between the kind of approach which appears to have been more helpful and the development of a fluent approach to practice is then examined. Before going on to describe the four unhelpful approaches, however, three points

117

require some clarification.

Firstly, the students' accounts suggest that in some cases their own approach to supervision may have played a part in generating an unhelpful practice teaching approach. In particular, some of the older, more experienced students who took part in the research tended not to reveal their learning needs in supervision because they found it difficult to adjust to their role as learners. That this was the case is supported by the fact that other students who took part in the research experienced a more helpful approach on the part of the same practice teachers. It may be, then, that to some extent at least the kind of practice teaching approaches encountered by the students were a function of the interaction between themselves and their teachers. On the other hand, in nine further cases where students had been placed with the same practice teachers there was some considerable coincidence in the extent to which the approaches employed by these teachers were helpful to them.

Secondly, it should be made clear that the approaches which will be examined in the following section of this chapter have been described as unhelpful not because the students themselves necessarily found them objectionable, although in most cases they did, but because they appear to have imposed constraints on the development of their practice.

Finally, it should also be noted that the four unhelpful approaches were not necessarily mutually exclusive. The implications of some of the combinations encountered by the students will be considered shortly. For the time being, however, they will be separated out and described as four distinct approaches.

Unhelpful approaches to practice teaching

Amongst the students who took part in the research two students encountered an approach to practice which was not dissimilar to the therapeutic approach described by Rosenblatt and Mayer, in that the difficulties they encountered in practice were attributed by their teachers to deficiencies in their personal development. This extract from the account of one of these students provides an illustration:

> By that stage supervision had completely broken down, so it wasn't all that much help at all. ... Basically, about half way through he gave me some critical feedback. I thought it was very badly handled. He sort of said things like most people who come into social work are damaged people and they have to learn to deal with their damagedness, and I don't think think you've learnt to do that yet. Then he said well you're going to have to work hard to pass this placement, and I thought is he saying I'm a damaged person, I've got a few weeks to sort my whole life out and I don't even know what's supposed to be wrong with me. I reacted very badly to that.

A third student had also encountered a therapeutic approach while on placement in the United States. In this case, however, the approach had consisted in a more general focus on her personal development rather than in the attribution of specific problems to particular personality defects.

A second unhelpful approach to practice teaching encountered by some students was very similar to the approach described by Rosenblatt and Mayer as an unsupportive approach, in that the students concerned found their practice teacher unhelpfully cold and aloof. For example:

> I found the sessions very difficult because of the way she was. She was a very serious, intense person. She came across as quite cold and detached like she wasn't putting a lot of herself into it. I can see that a lot of things I was doing then weren't right, but I felt the way she brought things up was very cold. It felt more like personal hostility rather than what can you learn from it.

While both the therapeutic approach and the unsupportive approach were comparatively rare, an approach to practice teaching which was not dissimilar to the constrictive approach described by Rosenblatt and Mayer was more common. In some cases the students' teachers had attempted to impose their own theoretical perspective on their students' work. For example:

> She had such a definite viewpoint, the psychoanalytical viewpoint, which I don't have the experience or knowledge to criticise, but it was the terms that stuck in my throat, having that imposed on my own particular work. ... She was very interested in his mother's early life experiences and in his own earliest experiences, whereas I didn't think it was appropriate to be exploring those things at that stage. There was just too much other stuff going on. Also I didn't feel particularly comfortable with doing it at that stage.

In a second case the intention of a practice teacher whose approach was perceived to be constrictive appears to have been to protect her student from undue stress at the beginning of a placement. In effect, however, she undermined his confidence by accompanying him on his first visit to his client and taking the leading role, leaving him feeling frustrated and unclear about his own role. In contrast, another student described her middle placement as 'spectacularly unsuccessful' because her practice teacher had allowed her to undertake very little work on the grounds that she might harm the people concerned.

While these variations on the constrictive approach are all documented by Rosenblatt and Mayer, an additional variation was described by some of the students who took part in this research. This involved the imposition of their practice teachers' own beliefs or ideology. In one case, for example, a student explained that her practice teacher was of little help because 'she was a born again Christian and that was imposed on everything'. Equally a student who had undertaken a community work placement felt that his practice teacher had attempted to impose her own ideology:

119

Between me and her it was like when two people are looking at things differently and neither person is prepared to hear the other. I felt I'd been labelled - 'typical social worker'. I know the way I reacted wasn't very helpful but she made me feel like everything I'd done before was worthless.

In other cases practice teachers had attempted to provide answers for the problems encountered by the students in practice and this too had been experienced as constrictive. For example:

I suppose my concern is that I don't particularly, I find the idea of the social worker just assuming that authority difficult. I talked it over with my supervisor and she was a lot more down to earth. I think she felt really I was being over sensitive: 'Don't worry, it will be alright when you get there. At this stage you're acting as much on behalf of the Reporter as anything else so you've got that authority, but also you're concerned and interested'. I suppose that was some help, but I'm not sure how much. It didn't really get to the heart of the matter as I saw it.

Although the constrictive approach was relatively common, the most common approach to practice teaching described by the students who took part in the research corresponds closely to the approach described by Rosenblatt and Mayer as an amorphous approach, in that it had lacked focus and direction. Of the forty placements about which detailed information was obtained this approach was encountered in sixteen cases. In some cases the approach again seems to have been associated with an intention on the part of a practice teacher to protect their student at the beginning of a placement. In response to their questions about what was expected of them, for example, two students reported that their teacher had told them: 'Just practise talking to someone to begin with', and 'Just get acquainted and tell me what you think'. This lack of clarity in the early stages of a placement was commonly associated with two more persistent approaches to practice teaching which lacked focus and direction. In the context of one approach supervision sessions appear to have consisted in detailed discussion of the students' cases during which possible explanations for the situations they encountered were 'thrown about' by student and teacher or 'batted off' their teachers by the students. The question of how the students might pursue their ideas further in working with the people concerned was not, however, addressed.

The second approach has some consonance with the approach described by Brodie (1990) as 'caseload management'. In the context of this approach supervision sessions appear to have involved the students in giving a summary of their work and an outline of their plans, which were then approved by their teacher with no further exploration. In some cases the practice teachers who employed this approach seem to have taken it for granted that this was what was required, a rather extreme example being provided by a student who had eventually questioned his teacher's approach:

> It was like chalk and cheese what I thought her job was and what she thought it was. I thought she should have been teaching me, but she said that was the university's job. She was just there to provide work experience and monitor what I was doing.

In other cases this kind of approach appears to have been agreed on by both student and teacher. This was most common when the student concerned was amongst the older, more experienced students who took part in the research, but it also occurred in some cases at the beginning of a final placement, on the grounds that at this stage a more 'consultative' approach was appropriate. Very typical of this approach was an approach to the students' written work which also involved monitoring rather than teaching. This student's response to a question about her written work provides an illustration:

> I didn't find the case notes much help at all. In fact that's something I would have liked more help with. My supervisor was very keen on me handing them into her every week, which was a bit of a chore, but as far as I know she never read them. I think it was more just to check I was doing them.

In considering the implications of these four unhelpful approaches to practice teaching, the experiences of three of the students who had been unable to develop a fluent approach to practice by the end of training are of particular interest, because the work they described at the end of training was very much more typical of the fragmented approach than that of the other ten students. While the other ten students had been able to resolve some, though not all, of the problems associated with the fragmented approach, these three students had been unable to resolve any of the problems they encountered. That they had been unable to do so seems likely to have been closely related to the practice teaching approaches they encountered, since all three students had encountered only unhelpful approaches throughout their education and training.

During her first placement one of the three students, who was amongst the older, more experienced students who took part in the research, had encountered an amorphous approach which she attributed partly to her own problems in adapting to the role of a student. This had been followed during her middle placement in the United States by a therapeutic approach and, during her final placement, by another amorphous approach, negotiated on this occasion between teacher and student. Her own assessment of these approaches illustrates the implications for the development of her practice:

> I think in the first placement it was me not recognising my learning needs, but that was balanced by the fact that my supervisor was the only social worker in the hospital and I felt I needed to take on my share of the caseload. ... In the States I worked very independently. Supervision was more reflective and more personal. We were looking more at my

feelings. That was interesting but there again it wasn't really focussed on the work. Now it seems to be the other way round. There's an expectation I would get on and do the job. ... It was my supervisor's idea. She thought because it's the final placement a consultative approach was appropriate, though I think there was probably some denial myself about what my learning needs were. I think I was flattered at first. Looking back on it though I think I needed to reflect back a lot more on what I was doing instead of this jumping about from one idea to another. In supervision it was more a matter of what had I done, what were my plans, fine. I mean I'm sure she would have told me if she disagreed, but I got the impression that all I had to do to qualify was stay six months and assimilate things.

While this student had attempted to deploy theory as recipes for practice during both her first and final placements, the other two students who had been unable to overcome any of the problems associated with the fragmented approach had deployed theory only with hindsight. During his first placement one of these students had encountered an amorphous approach which again seems to have been related in part to his own concern, as an older, more experienced student, to present a confident, capable front. This approach was followed by two further amorphous approaches. Towards the end of training the student identified a lack of focus on the problems involved in discussing difficult issues as a negative feature of both his first and second placements. Although he described his third practice teacher's approach as interesting and helpful, his account suggests that that it had consisted in an unfocussed discussion of ideas and sharing of feelings which had not enabled him to address the problems he was experiencing in raising issues he thought relevant with his client:

> I think what's been helpful in this placement is that my supervisor has always encouraged me to speculate about why people are in the situation they're in, why this woman has a poor relationship with her family, what her behaviour is communicating to the family, to the world. ... Probably the most helpful thing was being able to share some of the emotional difficulties you find you run into in terms of work with clients and feeling that your supervisor is saying this is alright, this is how I feel too.

Like this student, the third student had also encountered an amorphous approach during her first placement. In this case, although ideas had been 'thrown around' between teacher and student, the student's increasingly angry feelings towards her client had not been addressed and she had eventually withdrawn from her attempt to help. During her middle placement, she had encountered an extremely constrictive approach intended to protect the people with whom she was supposed to be working. Partly in response to the deskilling effects of this placement, in the student's view anyway, her third practice teacher had adopted a caseload management approach. Although the student had initially appreciated this approach, her overall assessment suggests that it was not helpful for the development of her practice:

> I think I was getting dragged along, not stopping to look at what was going on. I think perhaps, going back to supervision, I think if I'd been challenged a bit more that would have helped. I think partly because it is a final placement, and also because of the middle placement, because I'd written in my report that I needed more freedom than I'd had, I'd been left to get on with my own work. It's not as unsupportive as that sounds, but supervision has become very much work load management rather than supervision.

As was noted earlier, the remaining ten students who had not developed a fluent approach by the end of training been more able than these three students to resolve some, though not all, of the problems which were the hallmark of the fragmented approach. Their accounts suggest that this was associated to some extent at least with the fact that they had encountered a helpful approach to practice teaching during one, and in some cases two, of their placements. Equally, though, they had also encountered less helpful approaches during at least one placement. The variety of experiences described by these students preclude any detailed discussion of all ten cases. Three cases can, however, usefully be singled out for more detailed discussion in order to illustrate the implications for the development of their practice.

In one case the student concerned had encountered an approach which he experienced as both constrictive and therapeutic. On the one hand, he felt his practice teacher had attempted to impose her own psychoanalytic perspective on his work. On the other hand, she she also attributed his failure to approach his work as she suggested to personality deficiencies. In the students' own words: 'She put me on the dissecting plate too.' As this extract from his account indicates, his response was to conceal his feelings in supervision, along with the difficulties he was experiencing in practice:

> The thing that riled me was that she was also implying that I was emotionally split off myself, which - I mean I think there are probably some degree of splits in each of us, but there was some suggestion that I wasn't aware of some of my emotions. At points I got dangerously angry with her in supervision and I had to address that after a while, with myself. I changed my attitude to supervision after about six weeks and decided to be very much less open, because she implied that this 'split' was a worry for her about my practice.

During his first placement this student had struggled to make sense of the situation in which he was working in his own terms, and his approach had been fairly typical of the hindsight deployment of theory. In contrast a second student had attempted to deploy theory as recipes for practice. This extract from her account suggests that the rigidity of her approach was at least in part a reflection of the unsupportive approach of her practice teacher:

> My supervisor was very formal. I didn't know anything about herself, and supervision was very formal, very impersonal. ... It was very unhelpful. If you're accepted as a person then you can be yourself at work, whereas I took the social worker to work and left myself at home.

Although both these students encountered more helpful practice teaching approaches during their second and third placements, neither student was entirely able to overcome the problems they experienced during their first placement. It may be the case, of course, that they would not have developed a fluent approach even if their first practice teachers had been more helpful. Towards the end of training, however, the student who had encountered an unsupportive approach indicated that in her case at least the unhelpful approach she had encountered had contributed to her continuing difficulties:

> I don't think I was so cautious before. I mean in some ways that's good, but you need to be spontaneous sometimes, and that's what I've lost. ... I think the first placement had a lot to do with it. It was very much a process of withdrawal of me personally. The thing I keep saying is what happened to the person I used to be, which I know is part of the professionalisation process, but what happened to all the good and useful bits I used to have before?

Of the four unhelpful approaches to practice teaching encountered by the students the therapeutic and unsupportive approaches seem to have been the most unhelpful as far as the development of their practice was concerned. All the students who encountered these approaches indicated that their response had been to withhold information in supervision about the problems they experienced in practice, and to present a confident front. The disabling effects of these two approaches are most apparent, however, in the experiences of the one student who was just beginning to move away from the everyday social approach by the end of training. Prior to training this student had identified some concerns which it was her aim to address through training:

> Basically, it was just that I found working in the mental health field fascinating, and I could be very good at it, but it could be dangerous for me because I identified too much with people and got very drawn in. That's why I came on the course. I thought through training I'll learn the boundaries.

During her first placement, however, the student encountered an approach to practice teaching which she found cold and discouraging. Unsurprisingly under these circumstances, she was reluctant to reveal her concerns but had eventually done so when problems similar to those she had experienced prior to training began to emerge. In response her practice teacher had combined his unsupportive approach with a therapeutic approach by attributing the problems she described to a damaged personality. In the earlier stages of her work this student's approach had been very typical of the everyday social approach. After this supervision session, however, her account depicts one of the most extreme examples of the deployment of theory as recipes for practice obtained in the course of the research. This extract from her account suggests that her practice teacher's approach had played a part in this development:

> After that I decided to work on my own as much as I could. I started making myself present what I'd done in a positive light rather than telling him the problems I was having. At the same time though I was going through a bit of a crisis. I kept asking myself should I be on this course? Am I a social worker? Should I just pack my bags and leave? I came to the conclusion that what I'd do, I'd give it a damned good try and see what happened. So I sort of became a lot more determined, not just not to take any shit off people, but that if I was going to go and see people, then I was going to be listened to.

During her middle placement the student had encountered an amorphous approach which had enabled her to retreat from this position, back towards an everyday social approach:

> The middle placement was an easy placement really. It wasn't very challenging, but it gave me a chance to lick my wounds and get back to being myself again.

Consequently, the work she described at the end of her final placement had, to begin with, again been very typical of the everyday social approach. In the course of this work, however, she again began to experience problems similar to those she had experienced prior to training. Although she was very reluctant to raise her concerns in supervision, her experience of her third practice teacher eventually encouraged her do so:

> I was very wary of telling anyone about it because of what happened on the first placement. It was really important to me to get through this placement without anyone knowing. But in the end I thought well, he works with people with learning difficulties and he treats them like anyone else, so maybe he'll do the same for me.

At this stage the concerns she had identified prior to training began to be addressed, but as she herself concluded:

> It's frightening to think I could have got a different placement and got through the course without ever having addressed some of those things.

Again, it is not possible to know whether this student would have been able to develop a fluent approach to practice by the end of training had she encountered more helpful practice teachers during her first and second placements. Further evidence to support the view that the practice teaching approaches encountered by the students played a significant part in the development of their practice emerges, however, from the accounts of those students who were able to develop a fluent approach. As was noted earlier, five of these six students had encountered a helpful approach to practice teaching during each of their three placements. This approach is the focus of the following discussion.

A helpful approach to practice teaching

Like the approach described by Michael (1976) as an 'educational contract' approach, the kind of approach to practice teaching which appears to have been helpful in relation to the development of the students' practice was an approach within which emphasis was placed on identifying and addressing their learning needs. Unsurprisingly perhaps, this approach was also in many respects the antithesis of the four approaches described earlier. In contrast with the unsupportive approach, for example, those students who encountered a more helpful approach described their practice teachers as warm and reassuring, and as having a genuine interest in them. In turn, the students had felt able to discuss any anxieties they had about their placements or about the work they were allocated. This student, for example, described how her practice teacher's approach had helped allay some of her anxieties about undertaking statutory work:

> I think it was the fact that my supervisor, I liked her straight away. She came across as a very natural, friendly sort of person. So I felt comfortable saying it to her, you know, I haven't done this kind of work before. Well she knew that, obviously, but being able to discuss with her how nervous I felt about it, that really helped.

Equally, in contrast with the therapeutic or constrictive approaches, these practice teachers neither attributed their students' concerns to personal deficiencies, nor attempted to provide answers based on their own approach to practice. Instead they reassured the students that their anxiety was a natural reaction and that the purpose of their placement was to learn rather than to immediately demonstrate fully fledged competency. To the students this emphasis on learning usually came as a great relief, because from their perspective the need to demonstrate competence in the context of an assessed placement had loomed very large. Had their practice teachers only focussed on their role as learners, however, the students might have been left feeling deskilled. Instead, their teachers were concerned to help them identify strengths and skills they brought to their placement which might be of assistance to them, as well as areas they might address in the course of the placement. For example:

> I'd had a look at the assessment format they use and I'd thought, oh, this is going to be a lot about child development and childlessness, I hardly

126

know anything about those things. And then having thought that I went back to my supervisor and she helped me put it into perspective. 'What similarities does this have with work you've done before, what do you think you might be drawing on?' That was very helpful. I think because it was a specialist agency I'd assumed I couldn't possibly know anything, but once we'd discussed it in those terms I was able to see that I actually knew quite a lot that was relevant. So then it was a question of what else might it be useful to look at.

Having identified strengths and skills on which the students could draw as well as areas they might need to address, the focus of this approach to practice teaching was firmly on the particular pieces of work the students undertook during their placement. In the early stages of their work the students particularly appreciated their practice teachers' help in planning their approach. Again, however, their teachers did not impose their own ideas. Instead, they encouraged the students to draw both on their own experience and on the theoretical frameworks of which they were aware in order to identify potentially relevant lines of enquiry. Equally, though, the students' ideas were not simply 'thrown around' or accepted without further exploration as they were in the context of an amorphous approach. Rather their teachers challenged them to explain why they thought a particular area might repay exploration, how they had derived their ideas from the information available and how they might explore their ideas with the people concerned. They also encouraged them to extend their thinking by offering ideas of their own, in some cases by offering relevant books or articles, which were particularly appreciated. This student's description of her practice teacher's approach provides an illustration:

What I really appreciated about her approach was her openness to ideas. She wasn't taking one line - this is how it should be done. It was more a case of challenging discussion: 'What do you think, why do you think that, how might you act on that.' She'd listen and then pick up on things rather than saying this is how it's done.

This focus in the early stages of the students' work on enabling them to discuss their concerns, on encouraging them to identify their skills and strengths, and on challenging them to formulate and justify their own ideas was both a prelude to and a pattern for the way in which the students' work was discussed as it progressed. Throughout their involvement in the work they described those students who encountered this approach felt able to discuss the problems they encountered with their practice teacher without fear of personal criticism and in the knowledge that their concerns would be taken seriously. Most commonly, as has been seen, the problems encountered by the students revolved around the management of their interactions with the people with whom they worked, and around the legitimacy of engaging in particular activities. When they raised problems of this sort, their practice teachers did not attempt to provide ready made

127

answers. Instead they encouraged the students to reflect on why they found a particular situation difficult and to explore different ways in which they might overcome the difficulties they were experiencing. This student, for example, described how her practice teacher had helped her overcome the problems she had experienced in raising a difficult issue for discussion:

I had another case too, it was someone who was in prison and they were coming up for parole, and the offence was murder. I had to discuss with his parents how they felt about him living at home if he was paroled. I was trying my hardest to get it out, you know, to talk about it. There was no way. In the end his mother turned the tv up. That was me finished. I just left - thank you, goodbye. I was mortified when I got outside the house, but my supervisor was great about it. She said not to worry, it's not a disaster, we'll work on it and you can go back next week. ... First of all she started off with how am I in other situations, you know when there's something that needs uncovered or whatever. Then it all came out, I would never say anything to anybody, I would let people off rather than speak up. So then we brought it back to this case and we looked at how I might do it. We practised it - 'what if this, what if that'. So then I went out again, and it worked a treat. It did! They were just fine about it.

Equally, when the problems encountered by the students involved concerns about the legitimacy of some of their activities their practice teachers neither offered ready made answers nor treated the students' concerns as a personal problem. Instead, as this extract illustrates, they framed the students' concerns in terms of an opportunity to learn:

My supervisor was very good there. It wasn't like 'you've got a problem with authority' which I've heard some people say has happened to them. It was more like 'this is an opportunity to look at these things and make up your own mind'. ... The way he did that was he suggested maybe I should think of it as trying on a role, that as a student you could do that, that it didn't mean I was throwing all my own values or whatever out of the window. That was a very helpful way of looking at it I thought. It freed me up to look at some of the ways I might handle it, what felt comfortable and what didn't. I think to begin with I was a bit black and white about it if I'm honest.

Alongside this approach to the problems they encountered the students were continually encouraged both to develop and articulate their ideas, and to explore how they might make use of them in practice. 'Challenging' and 'questioning' were the words the students most commonly used to describe their teacher's approach, and these teaching methods seem to have been the centre piece of the kind of approach which was helpful for the development of their practice. In addition, however, the use made of written work as a focus for teaching was characteristic of the approach. While process recordings often provided a focus for detailed discussion, the students' routine written work was also used in helping them to develop skills in organising information. This student's description of her teacher's approach provides an illustration:

At first I sat down and panicked. I thought I couldn't write this up in four thousand words never mind a couple of paragraphs. I think I did about three rough drafts then I showed them to my supervisor. She was very good, she was always very constructive with things like that. She never made me feel stupid. She said I seemed to be getting the hang of it, but they were still a bit jumbled. She suggested it might help if I used more headings which I could take out once I'd got the information organised if they made it too bitty. That worked well. It took me a long time to begin with but I'm beginning to be able to do more of it in my head now. As I come away I'm already beginning to pin things on headings. Even at the time, when I'm with my client, I'm beginning to be able to use the headings to make links between things - that belongs with that, kind of thing. So then I can put that back to her - that rings bells with what you were saying earlier about so and so, sort of thing.

A second student described a different approach to his written work which he found equally useful:

That's something from my first placement actually. My supervisor showed me this key word system which I use all the time now. ...It's just a way of tagging the main issues and putting things together so you've got a structure for your notes. It helps you think in a more rounded way while you're working too. It stops you getting overwhelmed by all the information.

That there was a close connection between the development of a fluent approach to practice and this kind of approach to practice teaching is suggested by the consonance between the skills associated with fluent practice and those aspects of their practice teacher's approach which the students described as helpful. For example, the students' ability to draw not only on the theoretical frameworks of which they were aware, but also on previous experiences of practice and more everyday sources of knowledge in making sense of the situations they described appeared to be closely associated with their practice teachers' emphasis on encouraging them to formulate their own ideas and to analyse their feelings about the people with whom they worked and the situations they were in. Similarly, the development of their interpersonal skills appeared to be closely associated with the attention paid in supervision to resolving problems relating to the management of their interactions. Support for this conclusion is also, however, contained in the accounts of two of the three students who had been able to develop a fluent approach by the end of their first placement. Both students attributed the development of their skills at this early stage in their education and training to their first practice teacher's approach. Having again experienced a helpful approach to practice teaching during their middle placement, both students encountered a less helpful approach at the beginning of their final placement. Their accounts indicate that under these circumstances they had been unable to sustain the clarity which had previously characterised their work. In each case, however, a change of practice teacher in the course of their final placement had been associated with a return to their earlier clarity. These extracts from the two accounts in question illustrate the students' own perceptions of the influence of different approaches to practice teaching on the development of their practice:

> I thought at first the placement was going to be a disaster, but that's sorted out now. ... The practice teacher I had at first didn't actually work for the agency, and she didn't really know what the work involved. Supervision was very generalised, whereas I needed to focus more on the nitty gritty. For a while that was very frustrating. I felt I was just muddling along, but then she left and the supervisor I've got now has been brilliant. ... She's more like the other supervisors I've had. She makes you think about what you're actually doing. Apart from that hiccough at the beginning of this placement, I've been very lucky with the supervisors I've had.

And:

> I think to begin with I felt reasonably clear about what I was doing, and for a while I managed to hang onto that, but there was a stage in the work where I was beginning to lose sight of the issues. ... I think that was a lot to do with the supervision I was getting. It wasn't that I didn't raise the issues in supervision, but we just never seemed to get anywhere. He had a lot of work on his own plate and he just left me to my own devices, 'you get on with the work', because as far as he was concerned I was getting on ok. But the reason I went there wasn't to practise being a worker, it was to use someone to see what the issues were and build frameworks. With this supervisor we're beginning to do that and I feel these skills are coming together now. They were there before, but they were beginning to get disorganised and supervision wasn't helping with that. Both my first two placements were with what I'd call practice teachers rather than managers. They challenged me and made me think about what I was doing, and that's happening again now with this supervisor.

There is, then, some considerable evidence in the students' accounts to support the conclusion that the practice teaching approaches they encountered during their education and training played a significant part in the development of their practice. As was noted earlier, however, one student who had been able to develop a fluent approach by the end of training had not consistently encountered helpful practice teaching approaches. Her responses to questions about what had been helpful to her during her final placement suggest that in this case the unhelpful practice teaching approaches she encountered had been counter balanced by factors associated with her second and third placement agencies. The part played in the development of the students' practice by factors associated with their placement agencies is the focus of the remainder of this chapter.

The part played by the students' placement agencies

As has been seen, recent moves towards the accreditation of practice teachers have been accompanied by similar developments in relation to the approval of placement agencies. In 1989 CCETSW set out the criteria on which approval was to be based. In comparison with the attention paid to the training and accreditation of practice teachers, however, that paid to the approval of agencies seems somewhat sparse. The criteria for approval consist, for example, only in the following brief statement:

CCETSW approval of agencies for practice learning will be based on:

an agency policy commitment to (a) high standards of practice and (b) provision of high quality learning opportunities within an environment which encourages anti-discriminatory practice.

the existence of good systems for the support and guidance of practice teachers. (CCETSW, 1989b, p.5)

In their contribution to the workshop discussions which preceded moves towards the approval of placement agencies Harrison and Harris (1987) point out that it is no easy matter to decide either what level of support is required by practice teachers, or what constitutes a sufficiently high quality of practice. The difficulties involved perhaps account for the lack of detail in the Council's regulations. Equally, however, very little research which might provide assistance in this respect has been carried out. Although Michael (1976), Syson and Baginsky (1981) and Brodie (1990) all draw attention to the lack of resources and support available to many practice teachers, which Brodie in particular associates with a 'case management' approach to practice teaching, little is known about what other factors may add up to a helpful or unhelpful placement experience.

The information provided by this research is also inevitably limited, because the main focus of the research was on the students' approaches to practice and on their experiences of academic and practice teaching. Some information about the part played by factors associated with their placement agencies did, however, emerge from their responses to questions about what had proved helpful or unhelpful to them in undertaking the work they described. These responses suggest that four factors played some part in creating a helpful learning milieu: the contribution made to the students' learning by staff members other than their practice teachers; the pressure of work in the agencies concerned; the ethos and way things were done within those agencies; and the availability of role models. The students' contrasting experiences of their placement agencies are considered below in relation to each of these factors in turn.

The contribution of other staff members

In the opinion of many students, the people alongside whom they worked in their placement agencies had provided valuable information and support. In some cases this had supplemented a helpful practice teaching approach, while in others it had proved something of a lifeline to students who encountered a less helpful approach. One student, for example, described her colleagues as her main source of learning and support:

> I would have to say that any help I've had has been from colleagues. Since the first placement I've had very poor supervision. I mean I can see the need to be professional in supervision. I don't think supervision should be this collusive, pally thing some people get into, but at the same time you need to feel comfortable in supervision, whereas I felt I had to be on the defensive the whole time. So the fact that I had colleagues who were willing to discuss cases and listen to yours has been really important. Apart from the first placement I'd say everything I've learnt has been from colleagues, or just from myself.

In contrast, however, the people alongside whom another student had worked had compounded her practice teachers unsupportive approach:

> It wasn't just my practice teacher It was the whole team. From what I've heard it's very unusual for an area team. People do things in a very correct way. They don't even relax when they talk to each other in the coffee room. It seemed very formal, the atmosphere, and the students were somewhere down underneath the plebs. You were generally talked down to and patronised. It was assumed that you had no experience or knowledge to bring to the placement. There were some people who were different, but most people seemed to remove their characters before they came to work. I found it odd, and the other students found it odd. We spent a lot of time avoiding the coffee room because of the awful atmosphere there.

The pressure of work

The students' accounts suggest that the extent to which either their colleagues or their practice teachers had been of assistance to them was associated with the pressure of work in their placement agencies. The first student quoted above, for example, added to her description of the support provided by her colleagues the comment that she felt lucky to have been placed in an agency where 'people had time to talk'. A second student made a similar comment:

> Talking to other social workers is amazingly useful. That's the thing about the placement I had, people had time to talk to you about various

cases, whereas in the really busy teams people don't have that time.

As the student quoted above suggested, other students found that the pressure of work in their placement agencies had prevented them from making use of colleagues as a source of information and support. For example:

It helped that there were always other people in the office so if you were really stuck you could ask someone else. But there again everyone was always so busy. You're very aware there of the pressure people are under, and I didn't like to interrupt and ask things which to them might have seemed silly.

Several students, particularly those who had encountered a caseload management approach to practice teaching, attributed a less than helpful teaching approach to the pressure their teachers themselves were under. Comments such as this tend to support the conclusion drawn by Brodie (1990) that a caseload management approach may be associated with a lack resources and support:

I wouldn't want you to get the idea I blame him personally. I mean he was carrying a very full caseload himself, none of which were easy cases, if there is such a thing, and on top of that he was responsible for my cases too. So from that point of view he had to make sure he knew what I was doing in all my cases and that meant there wasn't a lot of time for anything else. I would say that was true of the supervision there in general, the supervision he would have been getting himself.

Agency ethos and organisation

The extent to which the students' placement agencies provided a helpful learning milieu also appears to have been associated with agency ethos and organisation. In response to questions about what had helped them in undertaking the work they described, three students indicated that a commitment to shared learning in their placement agency had greatly enhanced their own learning experience. As this student put it:

The approach in the unit wasn't a we are all so competent we can get on with it approach. It was very much a team approach. People sit down in the team meeting and say I'm having trouble with this issue, how have other people tackled it? The atmosphere's very enabling. It's not a case of if you can't do something you're incompetent. It's a case of if you can't deal with this maybe someone else has had the same problem, so you get the permission to discuss things, and that means you can draw on the expertise in the unit.

In contrast four students singled out an emphasis on displaying competence and coping abilities as having impeded their learning. For example:

133

I found them all very defensive and restrained. They didn't seem to help each other. There was one person I remember saying I've got this case and I don't know what to do about it, and I thought thank God somebody said that, because there seems to be an impression there that you have to know how to do it and that professionalism is the most important thing. ... Meaning keeping up the reputation of the team and being theoretically correct. It's not an atmosphere where you're encouraged to learn. If you can't do it you shouldn't be there, that's the impression.

In some cases a less than helpful learning milieu was associated not with an emphasis on displaying competence, but with an emphasis on the way things were done in a particular agency which left little scope for the students to develop their own ideas. Unsurprisingly perhaps, an emphasis on the way things were done was usually, though not exclusively, associated with area teams where much of the work undertaken was governed by procedural guide lines. In highlighting the restrictions imposed on the development of the students' own ideas by procedural guide lines it is not intended to imply that the provision of these guide lines was in itself unhelpful. On the contrary, several students commented on the support they derived when undertaking statutory work from the provision of clear guide lines, and in any case an ability to 'understand accountability and resolve to contain dilemmas between professional judgement and agency policy' is now a requirement of qualifying students (CCETSW, 1989a, p.20). In some cases, however, the rigid application of procedural guide lines diminished the opportunities available to the students for developing their own ideas. The most striking example of this emerged from the account of one student at the beginning of training rather than from the students' accounts of their placement experiences. Nevertheless it seems legitimate to present an extract from this account as evidence, since the agency concerned also offered placements to students:

I don't know how typical this is, but where I worked they had a tariff system for juvenile offenders and within that certain recommendations were regarded as higher on the tariff than others. I think the idea was to stop people getting caught up in the system too quickly. So rather than recommending supervision for a first offender, you would recommend the attendance centre, because that was the lowest point on the tariff. Basically that's how I arrived at my recommendation. It was a bit odd, the way it worked though, because it didn't really fit with what I'd written in the report about him being easily led. It's quite well known there that the attendance centre is a bit of a training ground for juvenile offenders, and most of the lads are a lot older than my client was. When it went to court the judge overruled it anyway. He thought going to the attendance centre would be putting him open to the influence of older lads, which is what I thought, but I was told I had to go by the tariff.

None of the students experienced quite this degree of restriction in the course of their education and training, but a variation on the same theme was not uncommon. In almost every case where the students were required to write a formal report in the course of their work, their practice teachers had encouraged them to model their report on reports which had been compiled by other members of staff. While the students very much appreciated this assistance in a task which they found particularly anxiety provoking, their accounts suggest that the 'model' reports to which they had access contained no reference to the social worker's own ideas. In turn they themselves were discouraged from developing their ideas about the situations they described. This extract from one student's account suggests that in some cases approaches to report writing had been governed more by the perceived expectations of other professionals than by the ideas of the social workers concerned:

> The reports I looked at really just covered the material facts. I asked a couple of people actually about that because it wasn't what I'd expected. The general impression seemed to be that the sheriff doesn't want some social worker's ideas, he just wants the facts.

That this approach to report writing was not unique to area teams is illustrated by the experience of a second student who had worked in a residential child care unit:

> I found it quite odd because the assessment report bore very little likeness to all the thinking I'd been doing. ... They're very practical things. I mean the reports differ, different members of staff have different styles, but basically I went on the type of thing that everyone else was writing, and very rarely was theory explicitly mentioned. It's more just a description of things that had been happening, any incidents, plus what she was saying about what she wanted to happen.

The provision of role models

The accounts of the students who took part in this research tend to support the conclusion drawn by Pithouse (1987), that social work is a peculiarly 'invisible trade'. As was seen in the previous chapter, when practitioners were invited into the academic setting to demonstrate ways of working this was very much appreciated. Only six students, however, described similar opportunities to watch people working during their practice placements. These opportunities were also highly valued. Moreover, as this extract indicates, the learning which ensued could make a significant contribution to the development of the students' practice:

> Working with elderly people was not something I had experience of so my supervisor arranged for me to 'shadow' a member of the elderly team. That was very useful. ... When we went to the day care unit it was really interesting watching the interaction and how he tackled that. It

135

was very illuminating to see that you can actually bring up some quite touchy subjects. ... First of all that it can be done, and that there are times that it has to be done, and secondly the importance of explaining why it has to be done. That you don't just sit down and say now I'm going to talk to you about your money. And thirdly the respect for somebody coming at an issue from a different point of view. That although to the worker it seems very clear and the system it's based on seems fair, to the client it doesn't seem fair. So recognising that as a reasonable perception to have. Not imposing what you think but looking at the different strategies open to that person. The way he handled that I thought was excellent. I learnt a lot there that turned out to be very useful in this case.

In summary, then, the students' accounts suggest that the features of a helpful learning milieu included the provision of a supportive, not unduly pressured environment, a focus on mutual learning, and the availability of role models. That these factors could contribute to the development of a fluent approach to practice is supported by the experience of the one student who had been able to develop a fluent approach despite encountering two unhelpful approaches to practice teaching in the course of her education and training. Towards the end of her final placement she described how the learning milieux provided by her second and third placement agencies had contributed to the development of her practice:

> This placement has been superb. Its value has been that it's taught me to organise my thoughts. I think that's partly because I've had quite a lot of cases, so you begin to see patterns, and partly because I've been able to pick up a lot in team meetings. I've moved from being able to see and understand things to being able to use that with people. ... The middle placement laid the groundwork really. I didn't do any family work, I did individual work myself, but I watched a lot. My joint supervisors were wonderful. Every time they saw a family the whole team watched, so I got to see a lot of work, and seeing that, and seeing it actually work, that has really been helpful with this placement. In this placement I've been able to put into practice what I learnt in the middle placement.

The implications for future research of both these findings and those presented in the preceding chapters are the focus of the following, concluding chapter.

9 Questions, answers and more questions

In the course of reviewing the work of previous researchers in the field of social work education it began to seem that research in this field invariably raises as many questions as it provides answers. It seems likely that this reflects the extent to which the field is under researched as much as it reflects the limitations of the methods employed. At any rate, this research also raises at least as many questions as it provides answers. The purpose of this chapter is therefore not only to examine the contribution made by the research in relation to the issues which it was hoped to address, but also to outline some of the questions raised which might be addressed through future research. While the first section of the chapter examines the contribution made and questions raised in relation to the aim of contributing to the development of methods for the monitoring and evaluation of social work education and training, the second section focuses on the influence of different educational activities on the development of students' practice.

Monitoring and evaluating social work education and training

As was seen in Chapter Two, the aim of contributing to the development of evaluative methods in the field of social work education was central to the funding proposal in which this research originated. Although the methods developed were very different from those originally envisaged, the main value of the research probably lies in the contribution made in this respect, and particularly in the construction of a typology of approaches to practice within which changes in students' practice as they progress through training can be understood. The description of the three approaches contained in Chapters Four, Five and Six arguably represents something of a break through, in that it is grounded in students' accounts of what they were actually able to do in practice rather than in prior assumptions about appropriate knowledge and skills. The research does, however, leave unanswered two important questions which require to be addressed through further research if the contribution made to the development of evaluative methods is to be consolidated.

Firstly, the extent to which the typology is generalisable to other students undertaking different courses of education and training remains unknown, and can only be assessed by replicating the strategy described here. It may be that this would result in the development of a rather different typology. For example, students who are changing career or returning to work in their forties and fifties may well have developed ways of understanding and managing their everyday social lives which differ from those depicted in the accounts of the students who took part in this research, the oldest of whom was thirty six at the beginning of training. The kind of everyday social approach described in Chapter Four may therefore not be relevant to older students. In turn, older students might respond differently to academic course content, with the result that the kind of fragmented approach described in Chapter Five may also not be relevant to these students.

Secondly, there is a clear need for future research to address the question of the extent to which any typology grounded in students' accounts of their work can be regarded as a hierarchy of performance levels. As was seen in Chapter Two, this might be achieved by combining an analysis of students' accounts with other sources of information, and on the basis of the evidence provided by previous researchers, clients' views about the service they have received from students seem likely to prove particularly illuminating in this respect. A recent study undertaken by Baird (1990) suggests, however, that the same care would require to be taken in ascertaining how clients' views make sense in their own context as requires to be taken in interpreting social work students' accounts. Baird sought to discover whether clients' views might be helpful in assessing students' practice. He notes that in some circumstances, for example where statutory work is concerned, clients may find any student's work unacceptable. Equally, he suggests that some clients may praise any student, whatever the quality of their work. A comparison of students' accounts of their work with their clients' views of the service received would therefore be a complex, though not impossible, undertaking.

The influence of different educational activities on the development of students' practice

The contribution made by this research to understanding of the influence of different educational activities on the development of students' practice lies in the light shed on three issues. These concern the use of theory in social work practice, the extent to which different academic teaching approaches enable students to make use of course content, and the significance of placement experiences.

As far as the use of theory in practice is concerned, the information obtained in the course of the research supports the argument put forward by previous writers such as England (1986) and Schon (1987), that to be of use in practice ready made theoretical explanations must be amalgamated and adapted to create custom made explanations for particular situations. In addition, the students' accounts suggest that these custom made theories cannot be constructed in the absence of a range of interpersonal skills which enabled them to communicate and check out their ideas in the course of their interactions with the people concerned.

As a corollary of the light shed on the use of theory in practice, the research has also provided information about the use of sources of knowledge other than the sort of knowledge which is usually described as theoretical. Hitherto, the other sources of knowledge on which social workers might draw have been described in rather vague terms such as 'intuition', 'practice wisdom' or 'common sense'. The classification in Chapter Three of the everyday knowledge on which the students drew in the absence of theoretical knowledge, together with the analysis presented in Chapter Six of the ways in which this everyday knowledge could be creatively combined with theoretical knowledge, therefore represents a significant contribution to understanding in this area.

This is not to imply that no further research is required. On the contrary, as was suggested earlier, further research might reveal a different relationship between theory and more everyday sources of knowledge were accounts of practice to be obtained from students with different background characteristics. Equally, although it is hoped that this research will provide a useful framework for the analysis of other social work students' accounts of their work, it would clearly also be of considerable interest were some different ways developed of conceptualising the information obtained. As was seen in Chapter Two, the analysis which has been presented here represents only one interpretation of the information obtained in the course of the research, and other interpretations developed from different perspectives might therefore have much to contribute.

The need for further research is also demonstrated by the contribution made by this research to understanding of the extent to which different academic teaching approaches enable students to make use of course content in practice. Although it might be tempting to suggest, on the basis of the information presented in Chapter Seven, that traditional approaches involving the division of course content into discrete subject areas and the dissemination of this content through the medium of lectures be abandoned in favour of more innovative approaches, it is by no means certain that such approaches are more effective. Rather, the influence of more innovative approaches on the development of students' practice requires systematic exploration and evaluation before any sweeping changes can be recommended.

The contribution made by the research in relation to the significance of students' placement experiences is arguably more conclusive, particularly where the influence of practice teaching is concerned. As was seen in Chapter Eight, the experiences of the students who took part in the research reveal an extremely close relationship between the practice teaching approaches they encountered while on placement and the development of their practice. The consonance between the kind of approaches which were helpful and unhelpful to them and the findings of previous research in this area suggest that claims for the validity of these findings can be made with some confidence.

Further research is, however, needed to address a question touched on but not properly addressed by this research; that is the way in which practice teaching approaches are established between teacher and student. In this respect some observation of the interaction between teachers and students, augmented by both parties' accounts of their supervision sessions, might prove illuminating. Although both Brodie (1990) and Gardiner (1987) obtained tape recordings of supervision sessions for the purposes of their research, their focus was respectively on the content of supervision and on identifying teaching and learning styles. Were tape or video recordings of supervision sessions to be analysed from the rather different perspective of the ways in which the interaction between student and teacher influences the content of supervision this might yield further valuable information.

Equally, further research is required to address the question of the extent to which students need the same emphasis on learning during supervision once they have qualified. As has been seen, the experiences of the students who took part in this research suggest that even in the final stages of training a clear emphasis on learning was required, and it seems unrealistic to expect that the acquisition of a qualification would in itself reduce this need. On the other hand, it also seems unrealistic to propose that the same emphasis should be provided, or indeed is required, throughout a career in social work. The extent of the emphasis on learning required by practitioners at different stages of their careers might therefore usefully be explored through the medium of a longitudinal study following students into qualified practice.

Finally, further research is also required in order to provide more detailed information than could be obtained in the context of this research about the part played in the development of students' practice by factors associated with their placement agencies. While the information which it was possible to obtain suggests that students' accounts of their placement work can illuminate something of what is involved in providing a helpful learning milieu, a combination of methods might again provide more information. For example, observation of agency organisation and ethos along the lines of that carried out in one child care team by Pithouse (1987) might usefully augment students' own accounts of their experiences.

Conclusion

In conclusion it is arguable that the research described here has demonstrated the value of qualitative research methods in exploring and evaluating the influence of social work education and training on the development of students' practice. These methods are, however, both time consuming and labour intensive, and it is difficult to see how the research can be built on in the ways suggested above, given that a survey undertaken by Richards (1985) has identified no fewer than ten sources of role strain already experienced by social work teachers. It seems rather unrealistic to add to this pressure the need to develop and make use of time consuming methods of evaluation. Although the solution to this problem clearly lies outwith the scope of this book, it seems legitimate to speculate about possibilities, and one possibility which increasingly appeals to me is that of establishing specialist research units to which both social work teachers and practitioners could be seconded. This would have two advantages. Firstly, it would create a link between social work education, research and practice the absence of which has been highlighted by a number of writers. Secondly, it would allow research of the type described here to be undertaken by teams of researchers rather than by individuals. As I struggled to make sense of the almost overwhelming amount of information generated by this research I thought with envy of projects such as those described by Becker et al. (1977) and by Oleson and Whittaker (1968), which employed teams of researchers to explore the processes of medical and nurse training. Not only would a team approach enable the work involved to be shared. It would also, I think, make for a flexibility and creativity in interpreting the information obtained which it is hard to maintain as a lone researcher. At present, however, ideas of this kind are purely speculative. What is more certain is that a great deal more systematic research than has hitherto been undertaken is required in the field of social work education, and that social work teachers cannot be expected to undertake this research to the extent to which it is required unless some way is found of freeing them to do so.

Bibliography

Badger, Douglas (1985), 'Building Bridges - The Transfer of Learning Between Field and Residential Social Work', in Harris, R.J. et al. (eds), *Educating Social Workers*, Association of Teachers in Social Work Education, Leicester.

Baird, Peter (1990), 'The Proof of The Pudding: A Study of Client Views of Student Practice Competence', *Issues in Social Work Education*, vol. 10, nos.1 and 2, pp. 24-50.

Barbour, Rosaline S. (1984), 'Tackling the Theory - Practice Dilemma', *British Journal of Social Work*, vol. 14, no. 6, pp.557-578.

Becker, Howard S., Geer, Blanche, Hughes, Everett C. and Strauss, Anselm L. (1977), *Boys in White: Student Culture in Medical School*, Transaction Books, New Brunswick.

Benner, Patricia (1984), *From Novice to Expert: Excellence and Power in Clinical Nursing Practice*, Addison-Wesley, Menlo Park.

Berger, Peter L. and Luckmann, Thomas (1967), *The Social Construction of Reality*, Penguin Books, Harmondsworth.

Bloom, Martin (1976), 'Analysis of the Research on Educating Social Work Students', *Journal of Education for Social Work*, vol. 12, no. 3, pp. 3-10.

Brodie, Ian James (1990), *Teaching from Practice in Social Work Education: An Analysis of the Content of Supervision Sessions*, Ph.D. Thesis, University of Edinburgh.

Burgess, Hilary and Jackson, Sonia (1990), 'Enquiry and Action Learning - A New Approach to Social Work Education', *Social Work Education*, vol. 9, no. 3, pp. 1-17.

Butler, B. and Elliot, D. (1985), *Teaching and Learning for Practice*, Gower, Aldershot.

Carew, R. (1979), 'The Place of Knowledge in Social Work Activity', *British Journal of Social Work*, vol. 9, no. 3, pp. 349-364.

CCETSW (1989a), *Requirements and Regulations for the Diploma in Social Work*, Paper 30, CCETSW, London.

CCETSW (1989b), *Improving Skills in Practice Teaching: Regulations and Guidance for the Approval of Agencies and the Accreditation and Training of Practice Teachers*, Paper 26.3, CCETSW, London.

Cicourel, Aaron V. (1964), *Method and Measurement in Sociology*, The Free Press, London.

Clark, Chris L. with Asquith, Stewart (1985), *Social Work and Social Philosophy - A Guide for Practice*, Routledge and Kegan Paul, London.

Clubok, M. (1978), 'Evaluating the Effectiveness of a Helping Skills Training Program', *Journal of Applied Social Sciences*, vol. 2, no. 1, pp. 33-41.

Corby, Brian (1982), 'Theory and Practice in Long Term Social Work', *British Journal of Social Work*, vol. 12, no. 6, pp. 619-638.

Coulshed, Veronica (1988), *Social Work Practice - An Introduction*, Macmillan, Basingstoke.

Cunningham, Catherine V. (1981), 'Performance Appraisal Tests for Staff Nurses', *Nursing Times*, vol. 77, no. 16, pp. 61-63.

Curnock, K. (1985), 'Educational Principles and Education for Social Work', in Harris, R.J. et al. (eds), *Educating Social Workers*, Association of Teachers in Social Work Education, Leicester.

Davies, Martin (1984), 'Training: what do we think of it now?', *Social Work Today*, vol. 15, no. 20, pp. 12-17.

Davies, Martin (1985), *The Essential Social Worker*, Gower, Aldershot.

DHSS (1978), *Social Service Teams: The Practitioner's View*, main authors Stevenson, Olive and Parsloe, Phyllida, DHSS, London.

Denzin, Norman K. (1978), *The Research Act*, McGraw Hill Book Co., New York.

Dingwall, Robert (1977), *The Social Organisation of Health Visitor Training*, Croom Helm, London.

Douglas, Tom (1989), *Group Work Practice*, Tavistock and Routledge, London.

England, Hugh (1986), *Social Work as Art - Making Sense for Good Practice*, Allen and Unwin, London.

Evans, D (1985), 'An Attempt to Establish a Learning Climate at the Outset of a Teaching Sequence', in Harris, R.J. et al. (eds), *Educating Social Workers*, Association of Teachers in Social Work Education, Leicester.

Evans, D. (1987), 'The Centrality of Practice in Social Work Education', *Issues in Social Work Education*, vol. 7, no. 2, pp. 83-101.

Fischer, Joel (1975), 'Training for Effective Therapeutic Practice', *Psychotherapy: Theory, Research and Practice*, vol. 12 (Spring), pp. 118-123.

Flanagan, J.C. (1954), 'The Critical Incident Technique', *Psychological Bulletin*, vol. 51, no. 4, pp. 327-358.

Gardiner, Derek W.G. (1984), 'Learning for Transfer', *Issues in Social Work Education*, vol. 4, no. 2, pp. 95-105.

Gardiner, Derek W.G. (1987), *Teaching and Learning in Social Work Practice Placements: A Study of Process in Professional Training*, Ph.D. Thesis, University of London Institute of Education.

Garfinkel, Harold (1967), *Studies in Ethnomethodology*, Prentice-Hall, New Jersey.

Gibbs, I. and Cygno, K. (1986) 'Reflections from the Field: The Experience of Former CSS and CQSW Students', *British Journal of Social Work*, vol. 16, no. 3. pp. 289-309.

Goffman, Erving (1971), *The Presentation of Self in Everyday Life*, Penguin Books, Harmondsworth.

Gould, Nick (1989), 'Reflective Learning for Social Work Practice', *Social Work Education*, vol. 8, no. 2, pp. 9-19.

Harris, Robert J. (1983), 'Social Work Education and the Transfer of Learning', *Issues in Social Work Education*, vol. 3, no. 2, pp. 103-117.

Harris, Robert J. (1985), 'The Transfer of Learning in Social Work Education', in Harris, R.J. et al. (eds), *Educating Social Workers*, Association of Teachers in Social Work Education, Leicester.

Harrison, David W. (1987), 'Reflective Practice in Social care', *Social Service Review*, vol. 61, no. 3, pp. 393-403.

Harrison, Alen and Harris, Val (1987), 'Accreditation of Practice Teaching', in *Accreditation of Agencies and Practice Teachers: Workshop Papers*, Complement to paper 26.1, CCETSW, London.

Howe, David (1989), *The Consumer's View of Family Therapy*, Gower, Aldershot.

Jenson, Alfred C. (1960), 'Determining Critical Requirements for Nurses', *Nursing Research*, vol. 9, no. 1, pp. 8-11.

Jordan, Bill (1978), 'A Comment on "Theory and Practice in Social Work"', *British Journal of Social Work*, vol. 8, no. 1, pp. 23-25.

Jordan, Bill (1982), 'Generic training and Specialist Skills', in Bailey, R. and Lee, Phil (eds), *Theory and Practice in Social Work*, Basil Blackwell, Oxford.

Keefe, Thomas (1975), 'Empathy and Social Work Education', *Journal of Education for Social Work*, vol. 11, no. 3, pp. 69-75.

Klemp, G.O. and McClelland, D.C. (1986), 'What Characterises Intelligent Functioning among Senior Managers?', in Sternberg, R.J. and Wagner, R.K. (eds), *Practical Intelligence*, Cambridge University Press, Cambridge.

Kopp, Judy and Butterfield, William (1985), 'Graduate Students' Use of Interviewing Skills From the Classroom to the Field', *Journal of Social Service Research*, vol. 9, no. 1, pp. 65-88.

Landy, Frank J. (1985), *The Psychology of Work Behaviour*, The Dorsey Press, Homewood.

Larsen, Jo-Ann and Hepworth, Dean H. (1982), 'Enhancing the Effectiveness of Practicum Instruction - An Empirical Study', Journal of Education for Social Work, vol. 18, no. 2, pp. 50-58.

Leighton, Neil, Stalley, Richard and Watson, David (1982), *Rights and Responsibilities*, Heineman, London.

Mayer, J.E. and Timms, N (1970), *The Client Speaks: Working Class Impressions of Casework*, Routledge and Kegan Paul, London.

Melia, Kath (1987), *Learning and Working: The Occupational Socialisation of Nurses*, Tavistock, London.

Michael, Gillian (1976), *Content and Method in Fieldwork Teaching*, Ph.D. Thesis, University of Edinburgh.

Miller, P.McC. and Wison, M.J. (1983), *A Dictionary of Social Science Method*, John Wiley and Sons, Chichester.

National Institute for Social Work (1982), *Social Workers - Their Roles and Tasks*, Bedford Square Press, London.

Nelson-Jones, Richard (1988), *Practical Counselling and Helping Skills*, Cassell, London.

Oleson, Virginia L. and Whittaker, Elvi W. (1968), *The Silent Dialogue: A Study in the Social Psychology of Professional Socialization*, Jossey-Bass, San Francisco.

Paley, John (1987), 'Social Work and the Sociology of Knowledge', *British Journal of Social Work*, vol. 17, no. 2, pp. 169-186.

Parlett, Malcolm and Hamilton, David (1972), *Evaluation as Illumination: A New Approach to the Study of Innovatory Programs*, Centre for Research in the Educational Sciences, University of Edinburgh, Edinburgh.

Patton, Michael Quinn (1980), *Qualitative Evaluation Methods*, Sage Publications, Beverly Hills.

Patton, Michael Quinn (1987), *How to Use Qualitative Methods in Evaluation*, Sage Publications, Beverly Hills.

Pithouse, Andrew (1987), *Social Work: The Social Organisation of an Invisible Trade*, Avebury, Aldershot.

Rees, Stuart and Wallace, Alison (1982), *Verdicts on Social Work*, Edward Arnold, London.

Richards, Margaret (1985), 'In Defence of Social Work Teachers', in Harris, R.J. et al. (eds), *Educating Social Workers*, Association of Teachers in Social Work Education, Leicester.

Rosenblatt, A. and Mayer, J.E. (1975), 'Objectionable Supervisory Styles: Students' Views', *Social Work (U.S.A.)*, Vol. 20, no. 3, pp.184-189.

Sainsbury, E. (1982), 'Knowledge Skills and Values in Social Work Education', in Bailey, Roy and Lee, Phil (eds), *Theory and Practice in Social Work*, Basil Blackwell, Oxford.

Sainsbury, E., Nixon, S. and Phillip, D. (1982), *Social Work in Focus: Clients' and Social Workers' Perceptions of Long Term Social Work*, Routledge and Kegan Paul, London.

Schinke, S.P., Smith, T.E., Gilchrist, L.D. and Wong, S. (1978), 'Interviewing Skills Training: An Empirical Evaluation', *Journal of Social Service Research*, vol. 1, no. 4, pp. 391-401.

Schinke, S.P., Blythe, B.J., Gilchrist, L.D. and Smith, T.E. (1980), 'Developing Intake Interviewing Skills', *Social Work Research and Abstracts*, vol. 16, no. 4, pp. 29-34.

Schon, Donald (1983), *The Reflective Practitioner*, Maurice Temple Smith, London.

Schon, Donald (1987), *Educating the Reflective Practitioner*, Jossey-Bass, San Francisco.

Schutz, Alfred and Wagner, Helmut R. (ed) (1970), *On Phenomenology and Social Relations*, University of Chicago Press, Chicago.

Shapiro, Constance H., Mueller-Lazar, Jeanne and Witkin, Stanley L. (1980), 'Performance-based Evaluation: A Diagnostic Tool for Educators', *Social Service Review*, vol. 54, no. 2, pp. 262-272.

Sheldon, Brian (1978), 'Theory and Practice in Social Work - A Re-examination of a Tenuous Relationship', *British Journal of Social Work*, vol. 8, no. 1, pp. 1-21.

Silverman, David (1985), *Qualitative Methodology and Sociology*, Gower, Aldershot.

Sowers-Hoag, Karen and Thyer, Bruce (1985), 'Teaching Social Work Practice: A Review and Analysis of Empirical Research', *Journal of Education for Social Work*, vol. 21, no. 3, pp. 5-15.

Stone, Mike (1985), 'The Induction of Students on Social Work Courses', in Harris, R.J. et al. (eds), *Educating Social Workers*, Association of Teachers in Social Work Education, Leicester.

Syson, L. and Baginsky, M. (1981), *Learning to Practise: A Study of Practice Placements in Courses Leading to the CQSW*, CCETSW, London.

Tyler, Ralph (1944), *Basic Principles of Curriculum Design*, University of Chicago Press, Chicago.

Waterhouse, Lorraine (1987), 'The Relationship between Theory and Practice in Social Work Training', *Issues in Social Work Education*, vol. 7, no. 1, pp. 3-19.